COMPUTERIZING WAREHOUSE OPERATIONS

Raymond A. Nelson

PRENTICE-HALL, INC.
Business & Professional Division
Englewood Cliffs, New Jersey

PRENTICE-HALL INTERNATIONAL INC., *London*
PRENTICE-HALL OF AUSTRALIA, PTY. LTD., *Sydney*
PRENTICE-HALL CANADA, INC., *Toronto*
PRENTICE-HALL OF INDIA PRIVATE LTD., *New Delhi*
PRENTICE-HALL OF JAPAN, INC., *Tokyo*
PRENTICE-HALL OF SOUTHEAST ASIA PTE. LTD., *Singapore*
WHITEHALL BOOKS, LTD., WELLINGTON, *New Zealand*
EDITORA PRENTICE-HALL DO BRASIL LTDA., *Rio de Janeiro*
PRENTICE-HALL HISPANOAMERICANA, S.A., *Mexico*

© 1985 *by*
PRENTICE-HALL, INC.
Englewood Cliffs, N.J.
First Printing . . . February 1985

Editor: George E. Parker

Library of Congress Cataloging in Publication Data

Nelson, Raymond A.
    Computerizing warehouse operations.
    Includes index.
    1. Warehouse management—Data processing.
I. Title.
TS189.6.N4 1985   658.7'85   84-22895
ISBN 0-13-163924-2

ISBN 0-13-163924-2

Printed in the United States of America

To the many men and women I have worked with—dedicated warehouse personnel striving to fill customer orders promptly and accurately. I hope this book will make their jobs easier and the results more rewarding.

Contents

14. Implementing a Computerized Warehouse System .. 220

Implementation Steps, 220 Training, 221 Documentation, 222 Design Factors, 222 Evaluation of Warehouse Options, 224 Development of Computer System Specifications, 226 Procurement and Installation of Warehouse Equipment, 230 Procurement of Computer Hardware, 232 Programming the Computer, 232 Testing and Debugging the Computer System, 232 Check Sheet for Implementation of the Computerized Warehouse System, 233

A Word from the Author . . .

I started to design improved distribution systems years ago, and a major effort was in the improvement of warehousing systems. The warehouse had to be designed using the constraints that were placed on it by the computer—there was little or no ability to have interactivity or real time computer power for the warehouse.

It often took an act of God for the computer to prepare picking documents in picking sequence. The addition of a location system had to be approved by the board of directors. So, we stumbled along, using the computer where possible, but mainly designing around the inputs that the warehouse received from the computer and being stuck with the outputs we were expected to provide the computer for financial and accounting controls.

All this changed with the advent of the mini-computer. Computer costs decreased startlingly; for example, a system put in for $50,000 in 1980 only cost $25,000 in 1984. A whole new vista opened up in improving warehousing efficiency.

As revolutionary as was the development of the forklift truck in the 1940's and 1950's, the computer gave opportunities for the warehouse in controls and work enrichment that are as important or more so than the development of the forklift truck.

A few years ago I modified my lectures at the American Management Association to include a course on computerizing warehousing operations. This was well received, as I did not just limit the course material to the computer or the routines that were necessary in the warehouse, but outlined the real requirements of warehousing, both for the computer and for the physical and people resources of the warehouse. I had found that Electronic Data Processing (EDP) and Management Information Systems (MIS) people did not know warehousing and, conversely, warehousing people were apprehensive, to say the least, about the computer. I therefore tailored my remarks to both groups—a little computer, a little warehousing—so that they would see the remarkable fit of the minicomputer with the warehouse.

In this book, I follow the same pattern. I have attempted to integrate the physical operation with the controls that are necessary for the computer to improve the operation.

This book will enable you to apply computer power to the warehouse—to increase productivity, to eliminate errors, and most important, to provide a rich, rewarding work experience for the warehouse employees.

1

Integrating the Computer with Warehouse Operations

Warehousing operations play an important part in the distribution of goods in the United States and in the world economy. Every manufacturing and commercial enterprise has as part of its operation the need to store materials and products, whether as raw materials for a production or assembly operation, finished products for customers, maintenance and repair parts for production plants, or office supplies for the administration and operation of the firm.

Hospitals must maintain inventories of pharmaceutical and surgical supplies, as well as linens, foods, and all of the other items necessary for the comfort of their patients. The local gasoline station must maintain inventories of tires, batteries, and other automotive components for its customers. The grocery store must maintain inventories of food products for its customers. So it goes on, back through the manufacturing and assembly operations, and to the producers of the raw materials for an industrialized society.

The warehousing operation, therefore, plays an important part in satisfying the needs of the customers of any enterprise. Adequate stocks of material must be inventoried, proper controls over the location of the goods must be maintained, and as customers order their needs from the warehouse, the warehouse must have good selection and shipping procedures.

1

As warehousing operations are a major element of most companies, the cost and efficiency of these operations must be controlled. These warehousing costs are:

Labor cost for the personnel involved in receiving, storing, and shipping the product

Space cost for the building, whether owned or leased.

Occupancy costs of lighting, insurance, heat, etc.

Cost of carrying the inventory

These costs are direct costs of doing business or servicing the end users of the inventories. They are often considered as an "indirect" cost of doing business and have, therefore, not been controlled as rigorously as the costs of manufacturing or selling.

The control of warehousing costs and their reduction, if possible, should therefore be a major aim for all enterprises, especially those with large warehousing operations.

WAREHOUSE OPERATIONS

The major functions of a warehouse are to:

Receive material

Inspect the inbound material for proper quality and quantity

Store the material and know where the items are

Pick or select the proper materials for a customer or end-user

Package the customer or end-user's order

Ship or deliver the order to the customer

All these basic functions of warehousing require close controls over the activities to be accomplished within the functions.

COMPUTER OPERATING
CONTROLS

In the past the computer has been used to provide detailed information to the management of the company. This has been a passive use of the computer and is illustrated by the masses and reams of paper that are handed to operating managers in an attempt to control the business and warehousing operations.

The computer *should* be used as an operating tool, integrated with the physical and control operations of the company. The computer can now be on-line and provide and receive information to update the records that are necessary to keep a warehouse operation under control. This can be accomplished in real time, rather than by batch operations as has been done in the past. When an order is placed on the warehouse, the inventory can be allocated to that order at the moment the order is entered; when the order is shipped, the inventory can be reduced; and when new material is received and stored, the inventory is available at that moment for new orders.

Another major advantage in using the computer is the ability to update various files at the same time. For example, when a customer submits an order to the warehouse, the files that should be immediately updated are the shipment schedule file, the inventory file for the items that the customer has ordered, the salesman's record of commissions due, and so on. The computer is now capable of entering data into these different files at the time the transaction occurs.

The computer can also communicate directly with the warehouse employees, using CRTs (Cathode Ray Tubes) or other input and output devices, updating records as transactions occur, and simultaneously updating a number of files that have an effect on the particular transaction.

THE PAPERLESS WAREHOUSE

The computer can be used to eliminate the tremendous amount of paperwork transactions that go on in the typical warehouse. These transactions start when material is received. A purchase order has to be reviewed to ensure that the receipt is correct. A receiving report is made out by the receiver showing the purchase order number, the item number, the quantity received, the carrier, the pieces, the total pounds, and so forth.

As material is put away, a record is entered by the warehouse personnel on the location of the material. As material is picked or assembled for an order, the warehouse personnel must write down the quantity picked and quite frequently the serial numbers or other numbers associated with the product shipped to the customer. As orders are checked, an inspector again must write down quantities, his or her name, and other information. When material is shipped, the shipper must again look at pieces of paper, check these pieces of paper, and transfer the product to the common carrier or vehicle that is going to move the goods. Data scanning equipment can allow the integration of mechanical and electronic equipment to communicate directly with the computer, thereby eliminating this cumbersome process of people reading and writing information that is already contained somewhere in the company's records.

QUALITY ASSURANCE

The elimination of errors prevalent in many warehouses is a key factor in the use of the computer in the warehouse. Whenever a person must read and write, there is the potential for an error to be made. If an individual puts the wrong item number down, for example, writing "1243" instead of "1234," and the record is updated incorrectly, there are two records that are in error, both the proper record and the record that was entered incorrectly. In many warehouse operations, the problems associated with correcting errors causes a considerable amount of lost time. As we shall see, the use of the computer can minimize this potential for making errors in the warehouse.

JOB ENRICHMENT

In the past we could hire a less educated person, give that person a forklift truck, or assign him or her to a picking operation, and the job probably would get done. In this day and age of technological advance, the warehouse personnel must be given the tools to perform the job accurately and correctly. It is difficult to find people who will take responsibility, have proper attitudes, and have respect for the work to be accomplished. All in all, we must upgrade the function of warehousing to attract professional people as warehouse personnel. Employees will not be satisfied if they are told just to put this material away, just to pick these orders, and just to package this material. They must be part of the total system and know their particular approach, their particular responsibilities, and their authorities with the operation involved. The computer can therefore be incorporated into the warehousing operation to give a higher degree of job enrichment and employee satisfaction for the firm.

EQUIPMENT CONTROLS
BY THE COMPUTER

There is mechanical and electronic equipment that can make the warehousing functions more effective and efficient. The reduction of labor in warehousing operations has been well documented in many warehouses in the United States and Europe. As the cost of labor increases, we shall see more mechanized and automated warehousing systems. The computer can be used to control these mechanical and automated storage and handling systems. Examples of these systems will be described in Chapter 10.

MAXIMIZING
UTILIZATION OF SPACE

The corporation or enterprise's investment in warehousing facilities must be properly used and must provide a proper return. Proper space utilization means using the maximum amount of the cube of the warehouse for storage and warehousing operations commensurate with good productivity of the warehouse personnel.

The computer can be used for maintaining the location

of all material in the warehouse and can provide measurements of the cube utilization for the total warehouse or for specific storage areas in the facility. More important, the computer can indicate where space is being used properly and by proper programming can increase utilization of space, indicating what material should be rewarehoused to more efficient storage cells.

INCREASING WAREHOUSING PRODUCTIVITY

Labor standards are necessary for the control of productivity in the warehouse. Standards can be applied to each of the warehousing operations so the individual supervisors in the warehouse can know their productivity and take action to continue a high productivity rate or take steps to improve a low productivity rate.

The computer can apply standards to the work content of a warehouse to enable the warehouse to be scheduled properly and to assign manpower to meet the work loads of a warehouse. This operating tool can allow first line supervision to schedule and control their activities to attain high productivity rates.

CUSTOMER SERVICE

The major objective of a warehouse is to supply service to the customers or users of the warehouse. Customers or user's orders are the lifeblood of a company. Orders must be processed to meet the delivery time requirements and item and quantity requirements of the customer. These service elements must be integrated into the physical operations of the warehouse and the computer can ensure that customer service needs are met.

A major customer service element is the timeliness of delivery of the customer's needed order. The warehouse has the responsibility to ensure that the order is shipped on time and that the warehouse work load must be scheduled to meet these necds. Information must be given to the warehouse operating staff for the orders that should be picked or assembled at the proper time.

Another major service element is shipping the proper items to the customer. The fill-rate is an indication of the ability of the warehouse to ship the proper material to fill customer orders. This means that proper inventories must be maintained in the warehouse to ensure that customers will receive a high percent of the items that they have ordered. A fill-rate of less than 90 or 95 percent will not yield happy customers. We can therefore see that proper inventory control is a major function that must be accomplished in most warehouses if the customers are to be satisfied.

Accuracy of order fulfillment is necessary to keep customers happy. A proper computer interface in the warehouse with the order checking or shipping function can help to eliminate errors and ensure that customer service needs are satisfied.

THE AGE OF COMPUTERS

Minicomputers have come of age. Whether a company will have distributed data processing or dedicated computers in the warehouse is irrelevant. Computer power must be made available to all employees of a firm to make their jobs easier and to ensure that they have the proper information to do the functions they are paid for.

The cost of computer power has decreased rapidly, and projections are that it will decrease further. Computers have become off-the-shelf equipment and are sold in the same manner as dryers, washing machines, and other appliances that require little knowledge of the internal workings and have minimum maintenance problems or down time. So we see that the computer should be applied to warehousing operations in order to:

Improve productivity
Control the physical operations
Maximize space utilization

Meet customer service in terms of time of delivery

Maximize the fill-rate for the warehouse

Keep employees happy

Increase productivity

THE COMPUTER-CONTROLLED
WAREHOUSE

Figure 1-1 shows the major files and programs for a computer-controlled warehouse. The major files are:

> *The Customer File* that includes the necessary information on the customers of the warehouse.
>
> *The Product Master File and Inventory File* that have the necessary information on the product line and stockkeeping units that are maintained by the warehouse, as well as the status of the inventory for each stockkeeping unit. (A stockkeeping unit, abbreviated as SKU, is àny discrete item that is maintained in inventory in the warehouse and that the customer can specify on an order.)
>
> *The Location File* that shows the location of the inventory in the warehouse by storage cell and SKU.
>
> *The Open Order File* that maintains the open orders on the warehouse and is used to schedule the warehouse operation.
>
> *The Transaction File* that maintains a record of all the physical transactions that occur in the warehouse and affords an audit trail of the material movements through the warehouse. The Transaction File is also used in conjunction with the *Standards File* to determine the productivity of the warehouse.
>
> *The Replenishment Order File* for open purchase orders or production requisitions can be necessary for proper receipts control for some warehousing operations.

Each of the warehouse operations can have a CRT, a visual display device for entering and receiving information from and to the computer. This allows the warehouse staff to use the computer as an operating tool for their particular work as-

FIGURE 1-1 Computer Files and Routines for Warehousing Operations

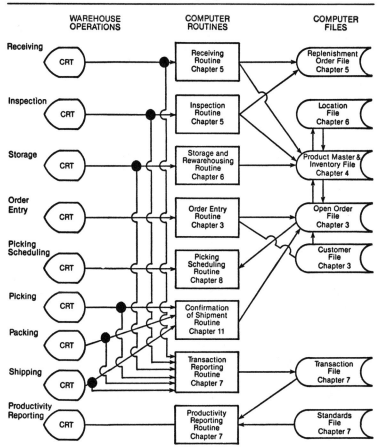

signment. In addition, printers for printing labels or reports can also be at the warehouse employee's work station.

The major program routines that are associated with the warehouse operations are:

The Receiving Routine transfers material into the warehouse.

The Inspection Routine ensures that the proper quantity and quality of product has been received by the warehouse.

The Storage Routine shows where the material is stored. If the material is moved from the initial location, we call it the *Rewarehousing Routine*.

The Order Entry Routine for entering customer or user's orders.

The Picking Scheduling Routine assigns orders to the warehouse for picking and packing (if appropriate).

The Confirmation of Shipment Routine confirms that the customer order has been picked correctly, packed, and shipped to the customer or user of the warehouse.

The Transaction Reporting Routine maintains all of the material movements through the warehouse and forms an audit trail of the warehouse's activity.

The Productivity Reporting Routine reports on the performance of workers in the warehouse.

Each of these routines and files will be discussed in the appropriate chapter of this book.

A check sheet ends each chapter to allow you to check off the necessary requirements for computerizing your warehousing operations and to ensure that your warehouse is using the power of the computer to:

Minimize costs

Maximize customer service

Have happy customers

Have happy employees

2

The Computer—Power at Your Finger Tips

The improvements that have been made in the past twenty years in computer technology have been staggering and should continue at the same rapid pace. The cost of computer power has been decreasing and will continue to decrease, thereby removing any economic constraints to wide use and allowing the computer to be used directly for the control of the physical operations in business, the home, and the warehouse.

The use of this power in the warehouse will allow improved physical operations by integrating the computer with automated and mechanized equipment, eliminating paperwork, eliminating handwritten entries through direct entry of data by warehouse personnel, scheduling work activities, scheduling the work load of the warehouse with consideration given to the availability of manpower and outbound carriers, and eliminating the calculations that have been necessary for the various functions of the warehouse.

WHAT IS A COMPUTER?

A computer consists of five basic elements:

1. *An input device*, generally a CRT, that allows the entering of information to the computer

2. *A program* to tell the computer what to do with the information

3. *A Central Processing Unit* that contains the program that instructs the computer on what to do, and the registers for electronically manipulating the data

4. *A memory* that contains the data

5. *An output device* that could be a CRT, a printer, or equipment that the computer is controlling

These five elements are the basic components that are necessary for a computer system: input, programs, CPU, memory, and an output device.

HOW DOES A COMPUTER WORK?

Figure 2-1 shows a simplistic drawing of a computer system that is receiving data on an item that is going into an inventory location. On the CRT screen appears the question: "What location are you going to put the material?" You enter "A-14," for that is the location where you want to put the material.

The computer puts this "A-14" into its register as the address of the file that it wants to find. It now asks "What is the item you are putting into this location?" You answer: "Item 1234." The computer puts this into its register in the CPU.

The computer then asks "How many are you putting into the location?" You answer "4 cartons." The computer puts this into the registers in its CPU.

The program now states for the CPU to enter the input data in these registers into the memory file for location A-14. The computer then searches the memory file, finds "A-14" and enters "1234 4" into the assigned fields of the memory file. This completes the input transaction.

Now, when we want to know what is in location "A-14," we tell the computer that we want to inquire into the Location File. This is a program and is presented on the screen. The computer knows, or has been programmed to know, that when we want to inquire, it must ask the proper questions: "What location do you want to know about?" We punch in "A-14." The computer then is programmed to search the memory for "A-14," by comparing "A-14" in its CPU register with the "A-14" that is in the Location File. When it finds "A-14" the CPU instruction is to take the data in the "A-14" file and transfer it to the registers in the CPU. When this is done the computer transfers these numbers "1234 4" to the CRT screen.

This is a simplistic explanation of how a computer works. By use of electronic circuitry that have registers, timing devices, transfer buses, and so forth, the transfer and manipulation of data are accomplished.

FIGURE 2-1 Data Transfers in a Computer

CRT SCREEN	CPU REGISTER	MEMORY FILE
At what location are you going to put the material?		
Enter "A-14"	A-14	
What item?		
Enter "1234"	1234	
How many?		
Enter "4 cartons"	4 cartons	
		Searches memory file for location A-14
		Enters product and quantity in location A-14 1234 4 cartons
	Job completed	
What location do you want to know about?		
Enter "A-14"	A-14	Searches memory for A-14
		Transfers contents of A-14 to CPU
		A-14 1234 4 cartons
Display on screen A-14 1234 4 cartons		

TECHNOLOGICAL ADVANCES

Computers have grown smaller and more powerful. With each generation of computers, technical expertise has developed more efficient and faster ways to transfer data back and forth from the input device to the CRT, to the memory, and out again. Undoubtedly, technology will increase the speed, increase memory capacities, and reduce computers' size and costs in the future

These technological advances have increased the usability of the computer so that the computers can be:

Faster and allow real-time control over operations

More efficient and allow many files to be updated at the same time interactively

Placed anywhere because of low power requirements.

REAL-TIME OPERATION

Records in the computer can be updated as transactions occur. In the old days, the computer was used to process data in batches. That meant accumulating all of the transactions to be entered and then processing them all at one time. Quite often this meant that the transactions were not entered until the evening shift or the end-of-week run of the transactions.

Now, as an entry is made, the computer will enter the transaction as it occurs and update all of the files at the same time on a real-time interactive basis.

INTERACTIVITY

Interactivity means the ability to update different files with the same information at the same time.

When material is received into a warehouse and put away, three separate files might be updated: The Purchase Order File to indicate that the material was received, the Location File for the warehouse to know the location of the material, and the Inventory File to indicate that the material is now in inventory.

As the warehouse inputs the receipt showing the purchase order number, item number, the quantity, and the location where the material has been put, the computer can make the proper entries in:

> *The Purchase Order File:* that the material has been received
>
> *The Location File:* the location of the material
>
> *The Inventory File:* the status of the inventory receipt

This ability to be interactive allows the warehouse to update on a timely basis the files that are necessary for proper warehousing operations and to ensure that all files have been updated.

INQUIRY CAPABILITY

Until the advent of the CRT only computer people had direct access to the vast amount of information that was in the computer. Now, with the proper programming and a CRT (and the proper security clearance), an individual has the capability to search for and instantaneously find any information needed.

CALCULATION CAPABILITY

A computer can calculate—add, subtract, divide, or multiply—using the registers in the CPU. These computations can take a computer less than a millionth of a second.

SEARCH CAPABILITY

The computer can have the proper search keys built into its memory files. In the examples just shown the computer can search by inventory location or by item number in the inventory

Location File. This allows the computer to search for and find information rapidly and present it in a manner that will be useful for the user of the computer system.

OPERATIONS vs. MANAGEMENT INFORMATION SYSTEMS

In the past the computer was designed for bulk processing of large quantities of data: payrolls, invoices, telephone bills, and the like. As the computer has become more powerful, it can now be interactive with various files and operate in real time for operational control over the functions of the business. In other words, where the computer formerly was used to present reams and reams of information, it can now be used to provide specific information on demand and rapidly.

INTEGRATION OF THE COMPUTER WITH EQUIPMENT

Equipment is now being designed that can be controlled by the computer. For a warehouse operation, this allows the integration of the computer with the storage and handling equipment of the warehouse.

WAREHOUSE CONTROL SYSTEM

Figure 2-2 shows a schematic of a simple warehouse control system. We see that

> The order entry routine will query the Customer File for the status of the customer and give the ship-to address and shipping instructions, while also inquiring of the Inventory File as to stock availability and if the inventory is available, allocating the inventory to the customer order, and entering the customer order into an Open Order File for warehouse scheduling—all at the same time.

FIGURE 2–2 Warehouse Control System

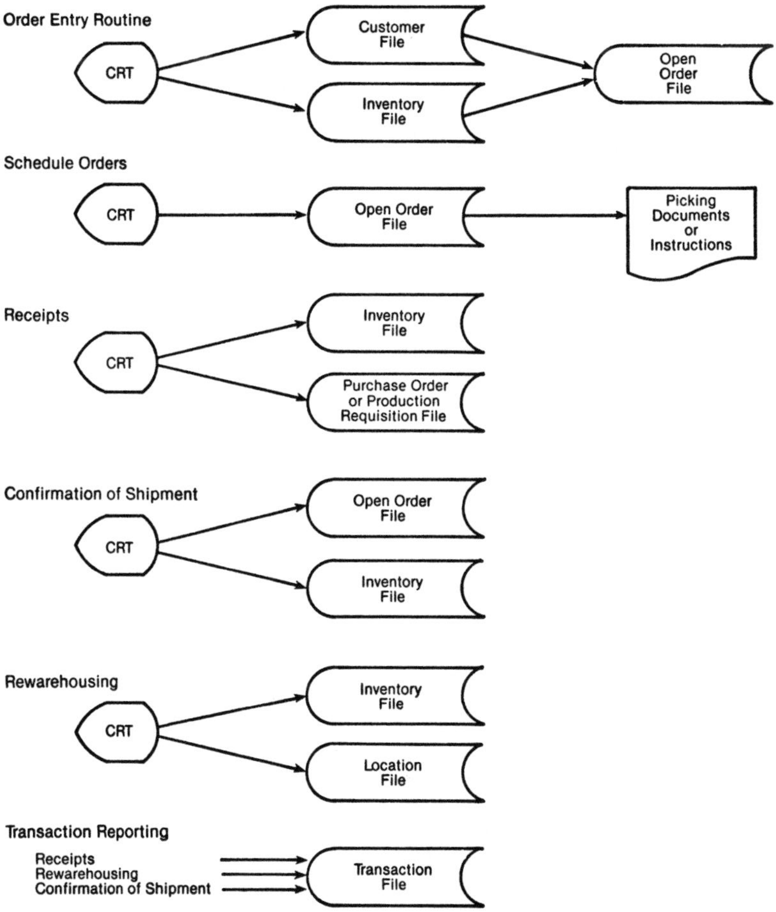

The Open Order File will be used to schedule orders by needed ship date and the availability of carriers and picking personnel. This will result in the preparation of the picking tickets, or labels, or electronic impulses to actuate an automatic picking machine.

The Receiving Routine will interactively update the Inventory File with the receipts and also update the Purchase Order or Production Requisition File with the quantity received.

The Confirmation of (picking and) Shipment Routine will update the Open Order File when the order has been shipped,

17

which will reduce the inventory and can also actuate the accounts receivable or user charge file.

The Rewarehousing Routine will record the movements within the warehouse in the Location and Inventory Files.

The warehouse Location File will record the location of received material, tell the Open Order File where the material is that must be picked for a customer order, or record the movement of stock to another location in the Rewarehousing Routine.

The Transaction File maintains a record of material movements and transactions throughout the warehouse showing:

 Receipts into the warehouse

 Rewarehousing or movements within the warehouse

 Picking orders

 Packing, if appropriate

 Shipments out of the warehouse

These are the main routines that must be considered in a warehouse operation.

3

Order Entry

Orders from customers, users, or production are the inputs that trigger a computerized warehouse system. This chapter will discuss the computer operations involved in the entry, acceptance, and processing of orders to allow the warehouse to assemble the items ordered, pack the material if necessary, and ship the needed material to the customer or end user. The elements of the Order Entry System are:

Order Receipt System. The input of the order from outside the warehouse.

Customer File. This defines the customer or user by their addresses, credit terms, account numbers, etc.

Allocation of inventory to the customer's order

Back-order preparation if necessary

Processing and acceptance of the order

Application of standard times to the order

The Open Order File

The Picking Document

ORDER RECEIPT SYSTEM

The warehouse can receive orders:

Directly from the customer by mail. The orders are mailed to the warehouse, where they are opened and entered into the warehouse computer system.

By phone from the customer. Many sales systems allow customers to call to place an order; other systems have sales service personnel at the warehouse or sales offices call the customer to solicit or obtain orders on a scheduled basis.

Direct transfer from the customer's computer to the warehouse order entry computer.

Transfer from a main-frame or other company-controlled computer. The order is entered outside the warehouse into a computer system, and the orders are electronically transmitted to the warehouse computer.

The major elements in the Order Receipt System are:

Identification of the customer. This assures that the customer is a bona fide customer or user who can withdraw product from the warehouse. It also confirms the customer's "ship-to" and "bill-to" address and any billing or costing factors.

Confirmation of credit of the customer. This procedure ties in with the company's accounts receivable system and credit system to ensure that the customer can pay for the merchandise. In other warehousing systems, this confirmation ensures that the user is entitled to the material and the costs will be charged to the proper account.

Confirmation of the item requested. This procedure checks to ensure that what the customer or user indicated was wanted is really what is wanted and that the warehouse stocks the item. This is important in many maintenance warehousing systems; the customer often knows what is wanted but is unable to provide a number or description that will allow the warehouse to fill the order.

Availability of inventory to meet the user's needs. This procedure has to be accomplished to ensure that there is stock available to meet the customer's requirement. This is often called "prepicking the order," which describes the operation of checking the inventory and allocating the inventory to the order *prior* to sending the order out to the warehouse.

Allocation of the inventory to the customer's order.
Most warehouses operate on a first-come–first-served basis for allocation of the inventory to the order. In a computerized warehouse system, the inventory can be allocated as the order is entered; no other customer can be assigned the allocated material.

Assignment of an order number. This mechanical procedure is necessary for warehouse control of orders and the identification of the order for operating and accounting purposes.

Confirmation to the customer that the order will be shipped. This is frequently unnecessary in fast reaction time order processing systems. However, if there is to be a delay, it is often necessary to correspond with the customer to confirm the order and supply the expected ship date.

Confirmation or deletion of items not-in-stock. Items not available for shipment at the time of order entry can be cancelled, put on "back order," or automatically scheduled for shipment the next time the customer orders. The customer usually has an opportunity to determine what course of action will be taken for items ordered that are not in stock.

Scheduling the order for shipment. The order is generally placed in an Open Order File and will be scheduled for shipment based on the customer or end user's need, the availability of stock, and the work load of the warehouse.

Preparation of picking documents or picking labels. This "hard copy" of the order depends on the system in use in the warehouse. For mechanized picking systems, the computer might just use the Open Order File and transmit it to the picking equipment.

Figure 3–1 shows a schematic of the Order Entry System. The order can be received at the warehouse in paper form, over the telephone for transcribing into the computer system, directly from a main-frame computer of the company or institution, or directly from the customer or end user's computer.

The various activities that must be accomplished are:

Confirmation of the customer or user using the customer file

Checking the item description using the Product Master or Inventory File

FIGURE 3–1 Order Entry System

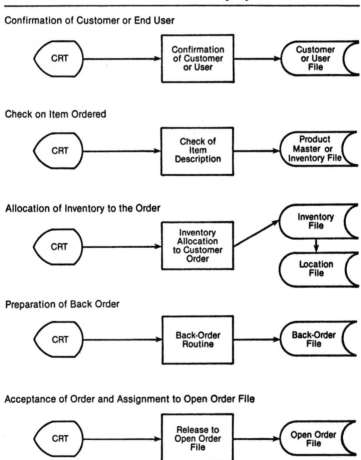

Allocating inventory to the customer order

Preparation of back order if items are out-of-stock

Accepting the order and placing it in the Open Order File.

After the order is shipped, the Confirmation or Shipment Routine will delete the order from the Open Order File.

THE CUSTOMER FILE

The Customer File is shown on Figure 3-2 in CRT screen format. The major data elements in the Customer File are:

The customer number

The customer name

The customer ship-to address

The customer bill-to address

Shipping instructions for the customer

Billing terms

Sales information: territory, salesman, and so forth

Back order handling instructions.

The Customer File can be entered automatically if the customer number is known. If the customer number is not known, a separate computer file in alphabetical order can be developed to assist the order entry clerk in finding the proper customer. A manual system for obtaining the customer number using a card file is often used by the order entry clerk.

The Customer File must be updated by Accounts Receivable for the customer's credit situation. A color code is often advisable:

Green. Process the order. The customer has good credit.

Yellow. Take care in processing the order. The customer has a credit limit.

Red. Do not process this customer's orders. Credit is bad.

FIGURE 3–2 Customer, Inventory, and Back Order Files in CRT Screen Format

```
                        CUSTOMER FILE

Customer Number XXXXXXX          Credit Code XXX
Customer Ship to                 Customer Bill to
Name  XXXXXXXXXXXXXXXXXX         Name  XXXXXXXXXXXXXXXXXX
Adr.  XXXXXXXXXXXXXXXXXX         Adr.  XXXXXXXXXXXXXXXXXX
City  XXXXXXXXXXX State XX       City  XXXXXXXXXXX  State XX
Zip   XXXXX                      Zip   XXXXX
Contact XXXXXXXXXXXXXXXXX        Phone XXX-XXX-XXXX
Billing Terms  XXXXXXXXXXXXXXXXXXXXXXXXXXXXXXXXXXXXXXXXXXX
Shipping Instructions  XXXXXXXXXXXXXXXXXXXXXXXXXXXXXXXXXXX
Sales Information XXXXXXXXXXXXXXXXXXXXXXXXXXXXXX
Back Order Handling  XXXXXXXXXXXXXXXXXXXXXXXX
```

```
                        INVENTORY FILE

Item Number XXXXXXX
Description  XXXXXXXXXXXXXXXXXXXXXXXXXXXXXXXXXXXXXXXXXXXXX
Package XXXXXXXXXXX     Unit/pack XXXX     Cube/pack XXXX
Weight/Pack XXXXX

Quantity      Quantity     Quantity     Expected     Receipts
on hand       available    allocated    date         quantity
XXXXX         XXXXX        XXXXX        XX/XX/XX      XXXXX
```

```
                      BACK ORDER FILE

Item No.   Order No.  Date      Cust. No.  Quan.   Package
XXXXXXX    XXXXXXX    XX/XX/XX   XXXXXXX    XXXXX   XXXXXXXX
XXXXXXX    XXXXXXX    XX/XX/XX   XXXXXXX    XXXXX   XXXXXXXX
```

The Customer File will be used to provide the Open Order Screen with the customer shipping and billing addresses and any special shipping instructions.

INVENTORY FILE

The Inventory File is also shown on Figure 3–2 and includes the Item or SKU Number, product description, and quantities on hand, allocated, available, and on order with expected date of receipt. The Inventory File is more completely outlined in Chapter 4.

As the item is entered into the computer in the Order Entry Routine, the quantities ordered will be allocated to the Inventory File. The computer will compare the amount available for shipment to the amount required by the customer. If there is sufficient stock, the computer will allocate the customer's requirements to the inventory allocated field and subtract this amount from the stock available.

If the inventory on hand is insufficient to meet the customer's need, the decision to be made will be:

Allocate what is on hand; back order the balance.

Allocate what is on hand; cancel the rest.

Cancel the line item on the order.

Hold the total order until the out-of-stock condition is corrected.

Each of these alternatives is dependent on the customer's policy on back orders and ship completes: some customers allow back orders, others do not; some customers want all items shipped complete, others will allow the transfer of the back ordered item to the next order. The customers back order policy can be maintained in the Customer File for reference during the Order Entry Routine.

The decision is also dependent on the order-filling policy of the company. Some companies allow back orders; others recognize the additional cost of split shipments and cancel back orders.

For a warehouse or stock room supplying a production, assembly, or a maintenance repair function, the picking of all the items ordered is necessary for the satisfaction of the user. It is difficult to assemble or repair a piece of equipment without all the parts. Communications must therefore be made to the user as quickly as possible if ordered items are not in stock.

BACK ORDERS

The control of back orders will therefore be a major subsystem for some computerized warehouse systems. Figure 3-2 shows the elements of the Back Order File. This file must be interactive with the Inventory File, Customer File, and Open Order File.

For reference to any inquiry by the customer and for proper control for the future shipment of the material back ordered, the file must contain:

The item or stockkeeping unit

The customer order number and date

The customer number

The quantity desired by the customer

The package quantity of the stockkeeping unit

Notification to the customer can be made by printing out a Back Order Notification for the customer. If expected receipts are shown in the Inventory File, the date of expected receipt and, therefore, the expected shipment date of the item can be included in this notification.

Back orders will become part of the Open Order File, or can be maintained in a separate file. Here, coding of the back order will be important if it is maintained in the Open Order File.

The back order should also be indicated in the Inventory File as an allocation to future shipments. The necessary information can be carried in the Inventory File so that when the material is received, it can trigger the Open Order File to release the back order.

Multi-items on back orders.   Another algorithm that could be necessary in the order scheduling system is the shipment of one item on a multi-item back order. To illustrate: suppose an original customer order has four items that cannot be shipped. These are put on back order. One item is received; the decision that must be made is whether to pick, pack, and ship this item, or wait for the other items to arrive. The options here are:

1. Ship the item.
2. Hold for a period of time and ship all items that have been received.

3. Hold until all items have been received.

4. Hold for a period of time until a designated weight has been attained to minimize transportation costs of the shipment.

If back orders are a major factor in the warehouse, then the back order routine becomes very important. It is hoped, however, that with the proper inventory control system, as defined in Chapter 4, back orders are at a minimum, thereby lessening the problem.

OPEN ORDER FILE

The order entry routine and allocation of inventory to the customer or user's order will allow the preparation of the order in the computer. Figure 3-3 shows an order as it would appear on a CRT screen and shows the data elements that must be carried in the Open Order File.

The Open Order File will be a working file of all orders on hand that have not been filled. (By proper coding, it can also include filled orders for inquiry purposes. For example, a filled order might be coded as filled with the ship date

FIGURE 3-3 Open Order Format on CRT Screen

```
                        OPEN ORDER FILE
─────────────────────────────────────────────────────────────
Our Order No. XXXXXX          Customer Order No. XXXXXXX
Customer Ship to              Customer Bill to
Name  XXXXXXXXXXXXXXXXXX      Name  XXXXXXXXXXXXXXXXXX
Adr.  XXXXXXXXXXXXXXXXXX      Adr.  XXXXXXXXXXXXXXXXXX
City  XXXXXXXXXX State XX     City  XXXXXXXXXX State XX
Zip   XXXXX                   Zip   XXXXX
Date Requested XX/XX/XX
                                                        Work
Line Item No.  Description  Quan. Unit  Loc.  Wt.  Cube  Min.
1    XXXXXXX  XXXXXXXXXX  XXXX  XXXX  XXXX  XXXX  XXXX  XXXX
2    XXXXXXX  XXXXXXXXXX  XXXX  XXXX  XXXX  XXXX  XXXX  XXXX
3    XXXXXXX  XXXXXXXXXX  XXXX  XXXX  XXXX  XXXX  XXXX  XXXX
4    XXXXXXX  XXXXXXXXXX  XXXX  XXXX  XXXX  XXXX  XXXX  XXXX
Total Items: XXXXXXX                          XXXX  XXXX  XXXX
```

and mode of shipment carried in the Open Order File for one or two weeks from the date of shipment to make inquiries simpler.)

The Open Order File will be interactive with:

The Order Entry Routine

The Customer File, if needed, for supplying and referring to customer ship-to and bill-to addresses, and shipping instructions

The Inventory File for availability of inventory

The Back Order File or Routine for items not in stock

It will include all orders that are on hand to meet customer or user's needs.

STANDARD TIMES
ON CUSTOMER ORDERS

For scheduling the warehouse order-picking work load, it is necessary to determine the work content involved in picking each of the orders. If the order has to be packed or assembled, these hours can also be included.

The determination of standard times for filling an order is presented in Chapter 7, Productivity Standards. For the Order Entry System, it is sufficient to say that a standards application routine will be necessary if the warehouse is to schedule the orders by using time standards.

This will encompass the:

Assignment of the time needed at standard that is dependent on each order. Travel time, review time, and so forth, must be allotted to each order.

Assignment of time needed for each line item on the order. This is work time that is directly related to the number of line items to be picked, such as search time, paperwork or control time, and so on.

Assignment of time needed to pick the physical unit. This is dependent on the characteristics of the item to be picked—

light, heavy, bulky, weighed out, and so on—and the unit picked—pallet, carton, inner pack, or piece—and can be included in the inventory file for multiplying the time value by the quantity to be picked.

The total time can then be determined and assigned for each order for scheduling the open orders into the warehouse work load.

LOCATIONS OF INVENTORY
ON CUSTOMER ORDERS

One of the prime requirements for an order-picking system is the location of the item in the warehouse. The location of stock can be indicated in the Inventory File and when the inventory is allocated to the order, the location can also be placed on the order. This allows the picker to go directly to the location when picking and minimizes the search time involved in picking orders.

The location algorithms and files are discussed in Chapter 6.

ORDER SCHEDULING
FOR THE WAREHOUSE

The Open Order File will be used to schedule orders for the warehouse picking (and packing) operations. This will be discussed in Chapter 8, Work Scheduling.

ORDER PICKING DOCUMENT

The output of the order entry and processing system will be the order-picking documents, picking tickets, or a computer batch for a mechanized or automated picking system.

Figure 3–4 shows a representative picking order for manual picking. This order shows:

FIGURE 3–4 Order Picking Document and Picking Label

```
PICKING DOCUMENT

                    XYZ Company
                  Invoice No. XXXXX

        Sold to                       Bill to
XXXXXXXXXXXXXXXXXXXXXXXX   XXXXXXXXXXXXXXXXXXXXXXXX
XXXXXXXXXXXXXXXXXXXXX      XXXXXXXXXXXXXXXXXXXXX
XXXXXXXXXXXXX, XX          XXXXXXXXXXXXX, XX
XXXXX                      XXXXX
Order Date XX/XX/XX        Customer P.O. No. XXXXXX
Terms XXXXXXXXXXXXX

                                    Unit      Extended
Item No. Description   Quan. Pack Location Weight    Weight
XXXXXX XXXXXXXXXX XXXX XX    XXXXX  XXXX.X  XXXXX.X
XXXXXX XXXXXXXXXX XXXX XX    XXXXX  XXXX.X  XXXXX.X
XXXXXX XXXXXXXXXX XXXX XX    XXXXX  XXXX.X  XXXXX.X
XXXXXX XXXXXXXXXX XXXX XX    XXXXX  XXXX.X  XXXXX.X
XXXXXX XXXXXXXXXX XXXX XX    XXXXX  XXXX.X  XXXXX.X

Total Items: XXXXX Total Packs: XXXXX Total Weight XXXXXX.X
              Standard Work Minutes XXXX.X
```

```
PICKING LABEL

              XYZ Company
Item No. XXXXXX Quan. XXXX Pack XXXX
Description XXXXXXXXXXXXXX
Customer Order No. XXXXXXX
Invoice No. XXXXXXX
Ship to
XXXXXXXXXXXXXXXXXXXXXXXX      Load
XXXXXXXXXXXXXXXXXXXXXX        Spot
XXXXXXXXXXXX, XX  XXXXX       XXXX
```

The customer order number

The ship-to and bill-to address

The terms

The shipping instructions

Each line item on the order will show:

The stockkeeping unit to be picked

The unit of pack—pallet, case, inner pack, piece (or other unit)

The number of units to be picked

The location of the stock in the warehouse

The order can include:

Standard times for picking (and packing) the order

Total number of pieces, cartons, inner packs, pallets

Total weight of the shipment (cube can also be applied if necessary)

The total cube and/or weight of the shipment

The mode of shipment or delivery

The invoicing information is frequently included on the picking document. The sales price of each item is extended by the quantity shipped, all line items are totaled, and any taxes or transportation charges are added. It is a good practice to combine billing with the picking documents, as it eliminates double handling of paperwork in the billing department. If this is done, it is called "prebilling" the order, since the costs can be applied as the order is entered, and transportation charges (if appropriate) can be calculated by the computer.

The picking label as shown on Figure 3–4 can be designed to include:

Item number, quantity, and pack description

Customer order number

Invoice number

Ship-to address

Outbound loading spot

It can also show, in machine-readable format, the outbound delivery vehicle or loading dock spot, as well as the customer order and invoice numbers.

The machine-readable label will allow automatic sortation of the case or package in the picking system. This alleviates the need for manual systems and can increase the picking rate by group or zone picking. These systems will be discussed in Chapter 8 on Work Scheduling and Chapter 10 on Automated Equipment Interfaces with the warehouse computer.

The order entry system must recognize the needs of the warehouse operation in scheduling orders (by adding standards), integrating with the warehouse operating plan for order picking (and packing, if appropriate), and the final delivery schedule for the warehouse.

CUSTOMER ORDER INQUIRIES

Sales personnel, customers, and users will inquire about the status of their orders. Provision must therefore be made for the rapid identification of the order, customer, and status of the order in the Open Order File. The considerations here are:

Identification of the customer.   An alphabetical file of customers that will give the customer number.

Identification of the customer order number with the warehouse order number.   This is a cross-reference file that can be entered with either number.

The display of the customer order.   This can be for reference or to make modifications and changes to the order. A complete order file should be maintained for past history and for inquiries of the status of completed orders. A completed order can be kept in the Open Order File for a period of time to allow order status inquiry.

SHIPMENT OF ORDER

The Confirmation of Shipment Routine will delete the order from the Customer Order File. This routine can be accomplished:

When the order is finally processed to shipping with the proper delivery or transportation mode.

When the shipment is put into the delivery vehicle or dispatched to the end user. This confirmation of shipment can be done at the shipping dock.

CHECK SHEET
FOR ORDER ENTRY SYSTEM

A check sheet for the order entry system is shown in Figure 3-5. It shows the elements that must be considered in the order entry system and the interfaces that must be established with the other interactive operating files and routines of the computerized warehouse.

Method of order entry.   This must be determined based on the sales and marketing procedures and the methods for receiving orders.

Order entry routine.   The editing of the inbound order to ensure that the customer or user is properly identified and that user charges can be made for the withdrawn material.

Assignment of inventory to the order.   This is the allocation of inventory to the order. It can handle substitution of other material and will include the establishment of a scheduled ship date.

Back order controls.   This is dependent on the back order practices of the company or institution. This includes the establishment of the back order file and the codings associated with identification of the back order, the assignment of receipts to the back order, and the determination of the shipping schedule for the back order.

Open Order File.   This will be one of the major operating files for the warehouse and will consist of all the open orders for the warehouse. It will be used for scheduling the picking and packing operations in the warehouse and will tie with the carrier or delivery system schedule.

Preparation of picking documents. This routine will be a part of the warehouse scheduling system, but must tie in with the order entry system. The documents that are necessary will depend on the method of transferring the order information to the manual, mechanized, or automated picking system of the warehouse.

Confirmation of shipment. This routine closes the open order upon shipment or delivery to the user.

Completed order file. This file is used for historical purposes, sales analysis by customer, by product, or other classifications.

FIGURE 3–5
Check Sheet for Order Entry System

Method of order entry
    Mail from customer or user
    Phone from customer or user
    Direct entry from customer or user computer
    Direct entry from company or institution main frame

Order editing routine
    Proper customer
    Proper credit or user charges
    Proper stockkeeping unit
    Proper package quantity
    Proper terms and sale conditions

Availability of inventory
    Stock available for the order
    Substitution possibilities
    Material on order and scheduled date

Back order controls
    Back orders allowed
    Coding of back order
        Open order file
        Inventory file
Open order file
    Customer identification
    Items, identification, package, quantity, locations

FIGURE 3–5 (continued)

Assignment of standards
Cube and weight

Preparation of picking documents
Picking order
Labels for identification of shipment
Computer to automated picking operations

Confirmation of shipment routines
Carrier or delivery mode
Scheduled date of shipment

Completed order file
Coding

4

Inventory Management and Control

The control over warehouse inventories is one of the major functions that must be accomplished by a warehouse computer system. Generally, the design of the Inventory File, the Product Master File, and the related receipts entry, order allocation, and confirmation of shipment routines must be accomplished first, as these are the major files and data transfers.

INVENTORY MANAGEMENT AND CONTROL

The proper control over inventories in a warehouse requires three levels of control:

1. *Inventory status.* This is the record-keeping function that keeps track of receipts, internal transfers, the location of goods in the warehouse, the material allocated to orders, and the final withdrawals or shipments from the warehouse.

2. *Inventory control.* The next level of control over the warehouse inventory is the determination of reorder points and quantities for proper replenishment of the items in the warehouse. The replenishment quantities must be determined based on the particular methods of procurement and replenishment times from vendors or from manufacturing facilities. This function must therefore interface with the procurement or production scheduling systems of the enterprise.

3. *Inventory management.* This highest level of control over inventories is the management function for determining the *proper* level of inventories in the warehouse that will provide proper customer service while minimizing the costs of carrying the inventory.

The inventory system for a particular warehouse must be integrated with the total inventory management system of the enterprise. Inventories are often the major asset of a company and must have proper financial controls, as well as proper physical controls for the warehousing operation. If the system is designed properly, however, the physical controls will allow better financial controls over the inventory. As financial controls are often on a main-frame, especially for a larger company or institution, the significant requirement for the warehouse computer system will be to supply the status of inventories, receipts, and withdrawals to the main-frame on a scheduled basis.

The main concern for a warehouse computer system is for proper inventory status—how much is on hand and where is it located in the warehouse. This could therefore be the main thrust of the inventory control system for a computerized warehouse.

Many smaller companies or warehouses that maintain specialized inventories, such as maintenance parts, office supplies, or parts for production or assembly operations, however, do not have the luxury of main-frame support. These warehouses must therefore have the ability to determine the proper inventory levels, reorder points, and quantities; to prepare procurement or replenishment documents; and to provide proper customer service at a minimum level of inventory.

Included in this chapter are the interface requirements that are necessary in a purchasing or production planning system, and a discussion of forecasting, determination of customer service levels, and the procedure for proper inventory management for the smaller, self-contained warehousing operation.

ELEMENTS OF THE INVENTORY STATUS SYSTEM

The major files of the inventory status system are:

The Product Master File. This file contains all of the pertinent information on every item or SKU that is maintained in inventory in the warehouse. For many systems, this information will be part of the Inventory File, eliminating the need for a Product Master File.

The Inventory File. This file maintains the status of inventory for each of the Stockkeeping Units in the warehouse, adding receipts as they occur, allocating stock to orders, and reducing the inventory as stock is withdrawn or shipped from the warehouse.

The Location Matrix File. The Inventory File can show locations by item or Stockkeeping Unit Number. This is adequate for many warehouses. In larger warehouses, however, it is necessary to have a Location Matrix File that will maintain inventories in location sequence. This file is discussed in Chapter 6.

These file structures will form the data base for the warehouse operation. Each item or SKU must be specifically identified for inventory and operating controls.

The major programs that will involve these files are:

The order entry and allocation system (Chapter 3)

The receipts entry system (Chapter 5)

The stock location system (Chapter 6)

The order scheduling and shipment system (Chapter 8)

The major algorithms that must be developed in conjunction with the inventory status, control, and management systems will be:

Reorder point and quantity determination

The forecasting system

Any interfaces with the main-frame computer for financial, purchasing, and production controls.

THE PRODUCT MASTER FILE

Every Stockkeeping Unit must be identified and described in unique terms as the SKUs will form the data base for the total warehouse computer system. For some warehousing operations this is a simple task, for others it is more complex, especially for those with large numbers of SKUs to be controlled.

The first order of business in developing the warehouse computer system is the development of the data base of stockkeeping units. Figure 4-1 shows the screen layout for a representative Product Master File. The data elements that must be included are:

The product class.   This indicates the "type" or "class" of product for the SKU's. It will be dictated by the type of activity the warehouse is maintaining inventories for and is illustrated by these types of products:

Hospital	*Grocery*	*Maintenance Parts*
Linens	Dry goods	Repair parts
Pharmaceuticals	Perishables	Operating supplies
Surgical supplies	Frozen food	Electrical items
Food	Candy	Wire and cable
Etc.	Etc.	Etc.

The product class can be necessary for proper warehouse controls over the type of storage, for keeping all items together

FIGURE 4–1 Product Master File

```
Item No. XXXXXXX            Product Class XXXX
Other Related Numbers   XXXXXXX    XXXXXXX
                        XXXXXXX    XXXXXXX
Description   XXXXXXXXXXXXXXXXXXXXXXXXXXXXXXXXXXXXX
              XXXXXXXXXXXXXXXXXXXXXXXXXXXXXXXXXXXXX
Short Description   XXXXXXXXXXXXXXXXXXXXXXXXXXXXXXXX
Specifications XXXXXXXXXXXXXXXXXXXXXXXXXXXXXXXXXXXXX
Unit XXXXXX        Package Quantity XXXXX
Other Package Quantities
            SKU XXXXXXX        Pack XXXXX
            SKU XXXXXXX        Pack XXXXX
This Package Length XXX.X    Width XXX.X      Height XXX.X
            Cube XXX.XX   Weight XXXX.X   Stackability XXXX
Transportation Commodity Code XXX.X
Seasonal Item Code XX
Hazardous Material Code XX
Shelf Life XXXXXXXX        Security Code XXXXXX
Storage Characteristics:      Type of Cell XXXXXX
            Stack Height XXXXXXX
Pallet Dimensions: Length XXX.X   Width XXX.X   Height XXX.X
Bin Item. Small XX   Loose XX   Weight Per Piece XX.XX
Standards   Receiving XXX   Storage XXX
            Picking    XXX   Packaging XXX
            Shipping   XXX
Usage History Code XX
Substitution Codes SKU  XXXXXXX  SKU XXXXXXX
Minimum Inventory Level XXXXXX   Maximum Inventory XXXXXX
Reorder Point XXXXX            Quantity XXXXX
Vendor or Sources   XXXXXXXXXXXXXXXXXXXXXXXXXXXXXXXX
                    XXXXXXXXXXXXXXXXXXXXXXXXXXXXXXXX
Price XXX.XX        Cost XXX.XX        Discounts XXXXX
```

for ease in picking orders, for procurement purposes, or for forecasting or financial accounting purposes.

The product class is quite frequently dictated by present marketing, operational, or past practices in the industry involved.

Item identification number. Each SKU must be identified by a unique number. This number can be assigned by the computer system for warehouse control purposes or it can be the catalog number that is used for marketing or operating control purposes.

The coding system can include the product class within

it, the unit of issue (as a code), or other factors that are necessary for identification of the item.

Other related identification numbers. The warehouse identification code number can be tied with other numbers that are associated with the SKU under consideration. These could include:

Vendor identification numbers

Customer identification numbers

Government or trade association numbers, and so forth

Description of the SKU. This should be a written description of the inventory item that identifies the specific item under consideration. It can be quite simple."Narrow line 8½″ × 11″ blue-lined pads of 100 pieces each" or quite complex, as for a repair part for a missile system.

The description of the item should not be limited in terms of length. It can give the proper information for procurement and, if necessary, should provide reference to a procurement or production specification. This could, of course, be maintained in a separate specification file.

For some warehouses this will be a complex task of assuring that each item is identified and properly described. *Any variation in the item identification should trigger the development of another SKU.*

Short description of the SKU. An abbreviated description of the item should be developed for inventory reports and CRT usage. This short description should be limited to 25 to 50 characters for ease in display or in reports. The use of abbreviations and codes will allow people to recognize the SKU quickly without the verbiage or detail specifications of the long SKU description.

Specifications for the SKU. This could be a computer file or a file of drawings, either physical drawings or on microfiche, that could be necessary for warehouse quality control purposes. A major factor here is the changing of specifications that occur as changes are made to the SKU. These will require a new SKU.

The unit.   The smallest physical unit or packaged quantity of the Stockkeeping Unit must be defined considering the units for financial accounting, the units in marketing catalogs, and the user's requirements.

The package quantity.   This can be in different units. For example, it can be in terms of individual pieces, or it could be in a carton of 12 units, such as a normal egg carton. Or it could be 144 egg cartons in a case, or it could be 20 cases of egg cartons on a pallet load, or it could be 40 pallets of cases to form a truckload.

The selection of the proper unit will be necessary for the integration of the SKU inbound quantity with the locator files for location of the SKU in the warehouse, the order-entry system for the allocation of stock to a particular customer or end user order, and for the financial status of the inventory.

The package quantity can be incorporated into the Inventory File as one SKU and transfers made as the package quantity changes. Or the SKU can be broken down into sub-SKUs based on package changes as the product moves through the warehouse.

In some systems, this will be a multitiered system. A truckload can be procured and will be stored in pallet quantities, then transferred to a case picking line, from which transfers are made to an inner-pack picking line, from which transfers are made to a unit or piece-picking line, and customer shipments made from each of the picking inventory locations.

The length, width, and height of the package.   This will be necessary for the location and space utilization routines, as well as the determination of outbound package or trailer size, and for packing and shipping routines. The dimensions should be in inches or in the metric system and should be accurate to the degree that is necessary to ensure accurate space utilization determination and cubing out outbound trailers or packages.

Changes to the package dimensions will be necessary in some applications. If this occurs, a sub-SKU or lot identification will be necessary.

For completely variable dimensions, for example, in break bulk applications where inbound quantities are to be allocated to users or customers, a subfile will be necessary. Every inbound shipment of the item will have to be sized at receiving or quality control inspection for inclusion in the product or inventory master file. From this data the computer can compute the cube of the piece, the carton, and so forth.

The weight of the SKU. The weight of the package must be determined on a sample basis or upon receipt into the warehouse. This weight can then be used for automatic costing of carrier shipments.

Transportation Commodity Code. This code is used for preparation of transportation documents.

For specific warehousing operations, the following information could be included as appropriate in the Product Master File:

Seasonal item. A code indicating that the item would only be inventoried during particular times of the year. Turkeys for Thanksgiving or Christmas Trees would be examples of seasonal items.

Hazardous material. Flammable or hazardous materials should always be kept segregated in separate areas of the warehouse away from normal material and with proper safety precautions.

Shelf-life items. Many items have a shelf-life and will have to be discarded if kept in inventory too long. These SKUs should be identified and the length of time in days defined so that each receipt can be identified on arrival in the warehouse and the shelf-life date computed. Each "lot" of product must then be kept separate in the inventory file (and the Location

Matrix File) for control. These SKUs must be carefully controlled in the warehouse to ensure that the first receipts will be shipped out prior to new receipts.

Security codes.   Items with high dollar cost or attractiveness to people have a tendency to walk out of the warehouse. These items must be kept in a security area.

Storage characteristics.   Some SKUs must be kept in temperature-controlled or air-conditioned storage. These SKUs must be able to be identified for the proper type of storage when the material is received.

Stack height.   Some product when placed on pallets or unit loads can be stacked one on top of another. Other product, however, because of the crushability of the cartons, cannot. Stackable pallets can be stored in one manner, but non-stackable pallets must be stored in pallet racks if the warehouse is to properly utilize the cube of the warehouse. The stack height must be identified, if important, in the Product Master File for these applications.

Pallet dimension.   Pallet size varies. This must be identified on receipt and the pallets put into the proper-sized storage cell in the warehouse.

Pallet height.   Pallet heights can vary by SKU. For storage purposes, this has to be identified when the material is received. Warehouses have various pallet rack heights, and a tall pallet cannot be stored in a pallet spot sized for a short pallet.

Carton dimensions and stackability.   Storage cells in the warehouse usually are designed for the product to be stored in them, for example, large, high, and wide shelving for large cartons, low and narrow shelving for smaller items. These can be defined for each SKU for proper storage location in the warehouse.

Bin items. A code can indicate small items or loose items (such as nuts, bolts, and the like) that must be stored in particular types of storage.

In addition, the Product Master File can include information on the item that will be necessary for the warehouse operating control:

> *Standards* for receiving, storing, rewarehousing, picking, packaging, and shipping can be maintained in the Product Master File, or could be included in a separate Standards File (Chapter 7).
>
> *Usage history.* Some items are very fast moving with high volumes. Others are slow moving with low volumes. A code can be developed based on past sales or usage history as to whether they are fast or slow moving. This is useful in the warehouse for the location of items in a forward picking line or for storage. The sales usage history could also be a part of another Sales History File for use by procurement and inventory management purposes.
>
> *Substitution codes.* These are items that can be substituted for the SKU and would be used in an order entry system.
>
> *Minimum and maximum inventory levels.*
>
> *Reorder points and quantities.*
>
> *Vendor or procurement source.* This could be a list of vendors or plants from whom the warehouse can procure the material.

Finally, the Product Master File could include information about the SKU that is useful or necessary for the accounting function or sales functions of the company. Examples of these are:

> *Pricing information.* The selling price per unit.
>
> *Costing information.* The cost per unit.
>
> *Discount information on pricing.* Discounts for large volumes.
>
> *Special pricing information.*

(These will not be considered in this book as they are generally beyond the purview of the warehouse operations and should be considered in the overall design of the company's financial control and invoicing system.)

Interactivity of the Product Master File. The Product Master File will be interactive with:

> *The Inventory File.* The Inventory File can have much of the information that is in the Product Master File, especially in coded format, or it could be completely interactive with the Product Master File, obtaining data when needed from the Product Master File.
>
> *The Order Entry Routine.* This interactivity can occur when the order is processed to ensure that the customer or user is ordering the proper item and to determine the correct item description.
>
> *Inquiry Routines.* For the proper item number and quality control requirements.

The Product Master File must be updated as changes are made to the SKU. It must be maintained on a current basis and, therefore, could be interactive with marketing, purchasing, engineering, and receiving routines.

The Product Master File could be printed out to provide a catalog of all the items in inventory at the warehouse.

THE INVENTORY FILE

The Inventory File will be the most important file for warehouse operations. It will maintain the status of the inventory in the warehouse for each Stockkeeping Unit, and will be interactive with:

> *The Order Entry System and Open Order File* for the allocation of stock to orders (Chapter 3)
>
> *The Location Matrix File* for locations of stock (Chapter 6)
>
> *The Rewarehousing Procedure* for internal movements of stock in the warehouse (Chapter 6)

The Confirmation of Shipment Routine for withdrawals of stock (Chapter 11)

The Receipts Routine for receiving and inspection of inbound product (Chapter 5)

This file, illustrated by the CRT format on Figure 4-2, will contain:

The item number. Each SKU will be identified and defined as noted in the Product Master File.

Short description of the item. A short description of the item in abbreviated form. (As opposed to the long, detailed description in the Product Master File.)

Package unit. The units per pack.

Reorder point and quantity and type of replenishment.

FIGURE 4-2 Inventory File

```
                          INVENTORY FILE
Item No. XXXXXXX
Short Description   XXXXXXXXXXXXXXXXXXXXXXXXXXXXXXXXX
Package units XXXXX
Reorder Point XXXXX     Reorder Quantity XXXXX
Type of Replenishment XXXXXXXXXXXX
On Hand XXXXXX
Available XXXXXX
Allocated XXXXXX
   Customer Order No. XXXXXXXX
   Quantity XXXXXX
   Date Ship XX/XX/XX

Location              Quan.    Allocated   Date     Employee
XXXXXXX               XXXXX    XXXXX       XX/XX    XXX
XXXXXXX               XXXXX    XXXXX       XX/XX    XXX
On Order
   P.O. No. XXXXXXXX
   Quantity XXXXXX
   Expected Receipt Date XX/XX/XX
On Order Allocated
   Customer XXXXXXXXXXXXXXXXXXXXX
   Order No. XXXXXXX
   Ship Date XX/XX/XX
```

Quantity on hand.   The quantity on hand in the proper units. This is the total quantity that is in the warehouse.

Quantity available for customer orders.   This is the quantity on hand after subtracting the quantities allocated to customer orders.

Quantity allocated to customer orders.   This is the quantity that has been assigned to customer orders. Subfiles in this file, or in a separate file for the allocated inventory, could include:

> Customer order number that has been assigned to the order
> Quantity and units of the order
> Scheduled ship date for the order

Quantity on order.   The confirmed quantities that are on order for the SKU. Sub-files associated with prospective receipts could be:

> Purchase order or production requisition order number
> Quantity to be received
> Expected receipt date

Orders on hand.   These can be allocated to future receipts by having a subfile for allocations of future receipts against confirmed orders for present or future needs. This subfile could contain:

> Customer Order Number
> Quantity
> Scheduled Ship Date

Locations of stock.   The locations of stock in the warehouse can be a designated picking location for the item in the proper package quantity or a random storage location. This field could appear as:

> Piece picking location

Quantity in piece-picking location
Quantity allocated with order reference

Inner-pack-picking location
Quantity in inner-pack-picking location
Quantity allocated with reference

Case-picking location
Quantity in case picking location
Quantity allocated with reference

Pallet-picking location(s)
Quantity in the location(s)
Quantity allocated with reference

In some situations, only the quantities involved need be entered in the location field without the allocation requirement. In high activity areas and when the computer system is controlling the replenishment of forward picking lines, however, it will be necessary to have the interactive allocation system.

Replenishment quantity for forward picking line. This is the quantity needed to replenish a forward picking line or designated location with stock from another location.

Multiple-item replenishment code. In a vendor-triggered system where more than one item should be considered for replenishment to obtain volume discounts, this will trigger a review of all stockkeeping units that can be ordered from that vendor for automatic replenishment of all the items.

The Inventory File will be interactive with the following:

The Product Master File. For certain situations where the information in the Product Master File is needed for processing with the Inventory File. This will be especially true when changes are made to the Product Master File, especially for quantities per unit, dimensions, weight, or for changes to the specifications of the SKU.

The Order Entry Routine. For allocation of stock to customer orders.

The Location Matrix File. For changes to the locations in the warehouse.

The Receiving Routine. For material received into inventory.

The Rewarehousing Routine. For material movement within the warehouse to increase space utilization.

Replenishment of Forward Picking Line Routine. For transfer of product from one location to another designated picking-line location.

The Inventory File should include much of the information that is defined in the Product Master File for ease in processing. Generally, the Inventory File will have the following:

Cube of the product
Storage characteristics
Standards for picking and other warehouse functions

UPDATING THE
INVENTORY FILE

The Inventory File should show an up-to-the minute status of the inventory in the warehouse. It will be updated with receipts, quality control releases, movements to storage, intra-warehouse transfers (rewarehousing), allocations to and shipments of customer orders, returned material (receipts), damaged material (withdrawals), and dummy transfers caused by errors and the rectification of the inventory records to actual inventory.

Receipts. The receiving routine will add inventory to the Inventory File if the receiving function also clears the receipt for quantity and quality. The receipt will be entered into the stock-available column, reducing the amounts on order and increasing the amounts available for allocation. Customer orders that have been waiting for stock will be released for shipment in conjunction with the Open Order File.

Inspection Routine. All material received and stored in the warehouse must have proper quality control and quantity checks. This is the responsibility of the receiving or inspection function. For some systems, receipts entry will trigger increases in inventory on hand, reduction in inventory on order, and the allocation of stock to nonfilled customer orders. For others, the quality control inspection will do the triggering of inventory additions.

Confirmation of put-away. When the storer puts the material away and provides the confirmation that the quantities are in the location, the location of the material can be put into the location fields of the Inventory File.

We therefore see that there can be three separate entries into the inventory file for a receipt. At receiving, the quantity is put into a noninspected file, after inspection the material moves to an inspected but not-stored file, and finally, when the material is placed in a storage location, the material is available for allocation to orders or for assignment to allocated orders. If this is accomplished in the inventory file, the CRT screen format would appear as on Figure 4–3.

Rewarehousing. As we shall see in Chapter 6, rewarehousing is important for proper space utilization in the warehouse. Material can be moved from large storage cells to smaller cells when the large storage cell is almost empty, freeing the larger cell for other material.

Here, two factors are important in the design of the warehouse operations system:

1. No material can be moved if an open order has been allocated to the location from which the material is to be moved.
2. The transfer of material in the warehouse must be reported to the computer for updating the location codes.

FIGURE 4-3 Inventory File (Elegant)

```
                        INVENTORY FILE
Item No. XXXXXXX
Short Description XXXXXXXXXXXXXXXXXXXXXXXXXXXXXXXXXXXXX
Package Units XXXXXX
Reorder Point XXXXXX      Reorder Quantity XXXXX
Type of Replenishment XXXXXXX
On Hand XXXXXX
Available XXXXXX
Allocated XXXXXX
    Customer Order No. XXXXXXX
    Quantity XXXXXX
    Date Ship XX/XX/XX

Locations              Quan.    Allocated     Date       Employee
XX-XX-XX               XXXX     XXXX        XX/XX/XX        XXX
XX-XX-XX               XXXX     XXXX        XX/XX/XX        XXX
Inspection
    Date XX/XX/XX    Quan. XXXX    Ref. No. XXXXXX
    Allocated:       Quan. XXXX    Order No. XXXXX
Receipts
    Date XX/XX/XX    Quan. XXXX    Ref. No. XXXXXX
    Allocated:       Quan. XXXX    Order No. XXXXX
On Order
    Date XX/XX/XX    Quan. XXXX    PO/PR No. XXXXXXX
    Expected Delivery Date XX/XX/XX
    Allocated:       Quan. XXXX    Order No. XXXXX
```

We will discuss this interactivity problem in more detail in Chapter 6 on the Warehouse Location Matrix and its effect on warehouse operations.

Order Entry Routine. Upon entry of orders into the warehouse, the Inventory File will be entered and the quantity ordered by the customer allocated to the file. The location from which the material is to be picked can also be determined at that time, which will effectively allocate the material, at the location, to the particular customer order.

For material that is not in stock, and if the customer allows a back order, future scheduled receipts of the SKU can be allocated to the customer order and create a back order. In some systems, this will trigger a Back Order File, which will contain the customer name, the customer order, the SKU, the quantity ordered, and the scheduled or requested ship date.

For inventory control purposes, the back order is really a future order on replenishment shipments.

Confirmation of Pick or Shipment Routines. After confirmation is made that the material is no longer in inventory and has been physically assigned to the customer, the Inventory File will be reduced by the quantity picked to the order. This can occur:

1. When the material is picked. Notification is received that the SKU has been picked to a customer.
2. When the material is inspected by an order inspector and found that the right SKU and the right quantity have been picked.
3. Upon packing the customer order and confirmation is received that the SKU and quantity have been placed into a package or container for that customer.
4. Upon movement of the material to a shipping acccumulation area.
5. Upon actual shipment of the material to the customer. This will be the final transaction to show that the SKU and quantity have been transferred out of the warehouse.

At least one of these transactions is necessary for withdrawal of material from the Inventory File. For some applications, the transaction that moves the material from one physical area to another can be used to report the withdrawal from the Inventory File.

Replenishment or transfer of stock from a location to replenish a picking line. This transaction transfers quantities of an SKU from one location to another location. It can also modify the package quantity of the SKU, for example, the transfer of cases from a pallet load to replenish a case picking line.

Cycle counts or physical inventories. Cycle counts or physical inventories can also modify the Inventory File by adjusting the computer ''book'' inventory with actual quantities on hand.

The inventory must be kept honest. There must be confirmations that the inventory is correct, either by cycle counts or by scheduled physical inventories. The changes made must be indicated as adjustments in the Inventory File.

INVENTORY STATUS

The inventory status can be determined by inquiry to the Inventory File. A visual display is shown on Figure 4–4 and indicates the activity of the particular SKU. Inventory status can be prepared as required by operating personnel.

A fundamental principle of advanced computer systems for warehouse operations is to eliminate paperwork. The major function of the computer should be to provide warehouse personnel with the proper information to do their job, mainly by use of visual displays. Lengthy computer reports should therefore not be necessary to show the inventory status of the warehouse and only exception reports should be considered. These could consist of:

Back orders by SKU to assist in expediting shipments

SKUs that are procured from the same vendor to assist in developing replenishment needs

FIGURE 4–4 Inventory Inquiry CRT Screen

```
                          INVENTORY STATUS

Description XXXXXXXXXXXXXXXXXXXXXXXXXXXXXXXXXXXXXXXXXXXX
Item No. XXXXXXX
Back Order Code XXX                 Expected Receipts
                          P.O.        Quan.        Date
On Hand XXXXXX           XXXXXXXX    XXXXXXXX    XX/XX/XX
Available XXXXX          XXXXXXXX    XXXXXXXX    XX/XX/XX
                         Allocated
                         Order No. XXXXX Quan. XXXX
                         Order No. XXXXX Quan. XXXX
          Location Code             Available      Allocated
Whse.  Aisle   Spot   Tier  Sub-Tier.          Order No.   Quan.
XXX    XX-XX  XXXX   XXX   XXXX      XXXXXX    XXXXXXX    XXXXX
XXX    XX-XX  XXXX   XXX   XXXX      XXXXXX    XXXXXXX    XXXXX
```

Listing of SKU sales activity for use in setting up and modifying forward picking lines

INVENTORY CONTROL

The Product Master File and the Inventory File and the related receiving, order entry, rewarehousing, and shipping routines comprise an Inventory Stock Status system, which must be incorporated in almost all computerized warehousing systems.

The next step for some warehouses is to develop the systems for Inventory Control. These include the elements for:

Determining the reorder points and quantities for all SKUs

Determining the replenishment lead time for all SKUs

Forecasting future demand for each SKU

Developing the procurement interface for purchased items or the scheduled needs from production sources

For some warehouse operations, the inventory control system will not be a part of the warehouse control system but will be maintained on a main-frame computer at the central headquarters.

PARETO'S LAW

Pareto's law simply states that:

About 20 percent of the SKUs in an inventory will account for about 80 percent of the volume, picks, activity, and throughput of the warehouse

and that:

50 percent of the SKUs in an inventory will account for *only* 5 to 10 percent of the volume, picks, activity, and throughput of the warehouse.

A relatively few items, therefore, account for the majority of demand on the warehouse. We will call these high-volume, high-activity items the "fast movers." They are the bread-and-butter items and must be controlled very carefully if the warehouse is to provide good service to the customer and users of the material from the warehouse.

The many, many items that account for a very small percentage of the activity in a warehouse are called the "slow movers," as they are replenished infrequently and generally stay in the warehouse for long periods of time.

The "medium" movers are those items remaining which account for about 30 percent of the SKUs and about 10 to 15 percent of the activity.

Figure 4–5 shows a representative Pareto curve for a real-life inventory for a retail operation. As can be seen from the curve, there are a total of 4,572 SKUs in inventory; of these:

125	account for 50 percent of sales, both in dollars and units
1,000	account for 80 percent of sales
3,000	account for 90 percent of sales
4,572	account for 100 percent of sales

The Pareto* curve is also called the 20–80 Rule, from the fact that 20 percent of the items account for 80 percent of the activity of an inventory system. The rule that 20 percent of the SKUs account for 80 percent of the activity should not be taken literally. We have seen situations where 30 percent of the items account for 70 percent of the activity and others where only 5 percent of the SKUs account for 95 percent of the activity.

Selection of units to measure sales demand is one of the problems associated with developing a Pareto curve for a particular inventory and usage situation. Physical units, that is, pieces, cartons, pallets, drums, truck loads, and so on, are the only proper units of measure. The unit of measure for a Pareto curve must be consistent—either all pieces or cartons or pal-

*Vilfredo Pareto, 1848–1923, Italian economist and sociologist.

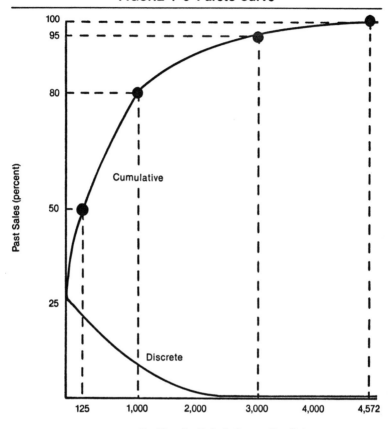

FIGURE 4–5 Pareto Curve

lets. The curve can be misleading if one mixes paper-clip-type items with typewriter-type items. Therefore, it is advisable to develop a cubic unit of measure that will take into consideration the package size. For many warehouses, more than one Pareto curve will be required to describe the activity of the operation, for example, a curve for pallet (or large items), a curve for cases, a curve for small items or pieces, and the like.

The Pareto curve can be developed using dollar sales volumes for each SKU. It is especially interesting for the sales or marketing department to see the many items that account for a relatively small share of the dollar sales. But dollars are generally *not* representative of the work content or activity of a warehousing operation. The development of a Pareto curve for profitability of SKUs in the warehouse, however, *is* an application that could prove of interest in developing the marketing strategy for a company.

Back to the warehouse. It is necessary that the Pareto curve, or curve of diminishing returns, be developed for the proper design of an inventory control system. The number of fast, medium, and slow movers must be defined, and with this information the proper warehousing system can be developed and the proper levels of inventory and customer service determined.

REPLENISHMENT OF INVENTORIES

Figure 4–6 shows the replenishment cycle for an SKU in inventory. Starting at Point A, a replenishment shipment for the SKU has been received and the inventory is at its peak level. As time goes by, inventory of the SKU is shipped to users or

FIGURE 4–6 Inventory Replenishment Cycle

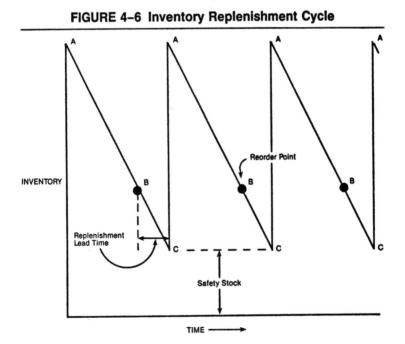

customers until we reach Point B, the reorder point, where it is necessary to order more material to replenish the inventory.

An order will be placed for more material, and time will go by, and more inventory will be shipped out of the warehouse until we reach Point C, when the material ordered will arrive into the warehouse and inventory will peak again. This saw-tooth curve will continue. We will reach the reorder point, order some replenishment stock, ship material to customers or users, and then receive the replenishment material, and so on, and so on.

Replenishment lead time. This is the time it will take for the replenishment shipment to arrive at the warehouse, once it has been ordered. This is the most important factor to define *for each SKU* in the warehouse. For some situations this is a standard time, but for many inventory systems it can vary depending on the vendor or production location, complexities of manufacture, and so on. It might be noted that fast movers are generally replenished more rapidly, while slow movers will tend to have longer lead times.

Once the replenishment lead time is known, the replenishment quantity can be determined based on the quantity needed to cover the demands of customers or users over the replenishment cycle.

For example, if weekly demand is 10 units and replenishment takes one week, you should start each week with 10 units and order 10 units to be received at the end of the week, thereby maintaining a very low inventory level because of the very quick replenishment time.

Real life is not based on such consistent demands; however, there are variations in weekly demand for many SKUs. If past weekly demands are plotted for a nonseasonal item, as shown in Figure 4-7, one can see there are variations in demand for the SKU. Also shown on the figure is a plot of weekly demands from the weekly curve. This shows a distribution of demand from the average. To cover the demands that are more than the "average," you must have additional inventory. This additional inventory is called the *Safety Stock* to cover unforeseen demands over the replenishment lead time.

FIGURE 4–7 Variations in SKU Usage

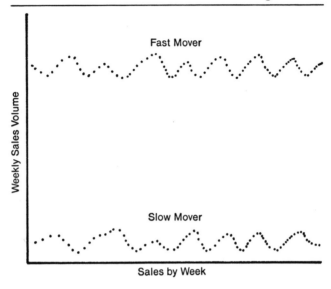

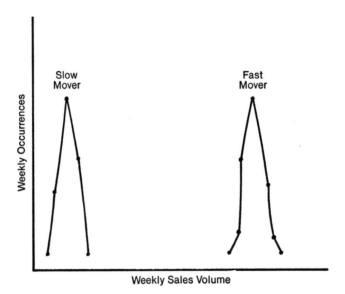

These calculations can be made in the computer to determine the proper inventory levels, safety stock, reorder points, and reorder quantities for each SKU in the inventory based on the forecast demand.

FORECASTING

The future is unknown; we can only estimate or guess at what the future will hold. But we can make educated estimates of what sales will be for an SKU in inventory based on available information, or information that we can obtain. There are five general methods of forecasting sales demands.

1. *Past trends.* The computer can keep track of actual shipments or sales demands for past periods of time. A pattern can often be detected for each item, and future demand can be assumed to continue on much the same as it has in the past. If past sales of an SKU have been 100 per week, every week, for the past 104 weeks, the best assumption is that it has a steady demand.

There are various methodologies for manipulating the data—basic trending as noted above, or exponential smoothing, which is a mathematical algorithm that weighs current sales more strongly than sales made some time ago. This method is especially good for items that are increasing or decreasing in sales.

Seasonal items can be forecast in this manner if history is available.

2. *Probability forecasting.* This method is based on the making of usage estimates by knowledgeable sales managers or users involved in the actual sale or usage of the unit. A "pessimistic" sales estimate can be made that would have 100 percent probability; then a "most likely" estimate of sales with a 50 percent probability; and finally an "optimistic" sales estimate with a 5 to 10 percent probability of attainment. This will create a probability curve of forecast sales, and by using the potential rewards of having inventory and making the sales weighted against the probability of not having inventory and not making the sales, a decision can be made on the proper inventory levels.

3. *Distribution requirements planning.* In this methodology, an estimate of the sales demand is made for the average weekly sales. Then the inventory replenishment plan is developed for the future showing the "saw-tooth" replenishment curve. The computer tracks the actual performance against the idealized curve and, as changes are detected, will automatically increase or decrease the inventory based on the replenishment lead times. The computer can also indicate where changes should be made to the replenishment lead times based on actual performance of the replenishment system.

4. *User requirements dictate the demand.* In many inventory systems, demand on the inventory is dictated by the customer or end user. For example:

> A tire manufacturer with a contract with an automotive manufacturer will know the number of automobiles that the manufacturer is producing per day and therefore has a contractual commitment to meet these demands on a scheduled basis. The only error here is if the automobile manufacturer reduces, or increases, the amount of production.
>
> A surgical item in a hospital is dependent on the number of surgical operations that will be performed each week in the hospital. This is generally predictable based on past history of surgical operations at the hospital.
>
> Maintenance parts usage can be predicted based on past history or the probability of failure of the part under consideration. Most manufacturers of equipment will have made a probability of failure analysis for each part of their equipment. For example, in an automobile the probability of failure of brake drums is based on the miles driven and is generally higher than the failure of the axle.

5. *Two-bin system.* A two-bin system is excellent for slow-moving items. When material is received, a portion of the material is designated as the stock necessary to be on hand at the reorder point. As material is used, the warehouse will break into this batch of material. When this occurs, material will be reordered.

As usage increases, material will have to be ordered more frequently. If usage decreases, material will have to be ordered less frequently. By tracking this time element, the reorder quantity can be increased or decreased to get the correct balance between the order quantity and the ordering cycle time.

It should be emphasized that there are major differences in forecasting demands for fast, medium, and slow-moving items in an inventory system.

Fast movers are generally fairly consistent in their demands. There can be seasonal peaks that will repeat themselves. In addition, as fast movers can be generally replenished more rapidly than other items in inventory, corrections can be quickly made if future demand is under-estimated or over-estimated.

Medium movers are the most difficult to forecast and therefore the most difficult inventories to control. Some medium movers will have consistent demand, and they are forecast in the same manner as the fast movers. But, for many of these types of SKU, demand over time is quite variable with peaks and valleys. These items might be best controlled with an exponential smoothing system or a distribution-requirements planning system.

Slow movers, while having variations in demand, do not have the high peaks and low valleys of demand the medium movers have, as their sale volume per SKU is relatively very low. An error in forecasting will show up in extremely high levels of inventory. If the item is a continuous mover, however, the effect on total inventory cost is minimized as the total value of the inventory is small, as compared with medium- and fast-moving SKUs in the system.

The forecasting algorithms to be used in a computerized warehouse inventory control system will depend on the marketing strategies of the company, the needs of users and customers, the predictability of demands, and so forth.

PROCUREMENT INTERFACE

Material can be replenished to the warehouse from either vendor sources or manufacturing plants that are tied with the company or the institution. In a "push" inventory replenishment system, the warehouse accepts what is provided, and the inventory control responsibility and authority are outside the warehouse's responsibility. In a "pull" system, the warehouse must order the material to replenish stock.

The warehouse in a pull system must make its requirements known to the vendors and a Purchase Order has to be communicated to the vendor, or in the case of production, a Production Request must be communicated to the production planning and control system. In either case the warehouse inventory control system triggers the procurement.

Purchasing system interface   When a reorder point is reached the inventory control system must interface with the purchasing system. The first problem to be attacked is, from whom can we buy this item? This information is the responsibility of the purchasing staff and a file can be developed by vendor and their merchandise. This can then be coded into the Inventory File or Product Master File to indicate those vendors who are supplying the SKU.

The next need is to obtain bids from vendors on the particular SKU and to make the decision to buy this material from a particular vendor at a particular price. A Purchase Order then must be made.

When the material is received against the Purchase Order number, the purchasing system is relieved of the order and an interface occurs with the accounts payable function.

Figure 4–8 shows an illustrative interactive purchasing system tied with the warehouse inventory control system. The files and routines necessary are:

> The Vendor Performance File, which shows the purchase order history and the performance of the vendor in meeting delivery dates and quality of items for each vendor.
>
> The SKU history file, showing vendors used, costs, quantities, and vendor performance.
>
> The writing, approval, and transmission of the Purchase Order to the vendor.

FIGURE 4-8 Purchasing Interface

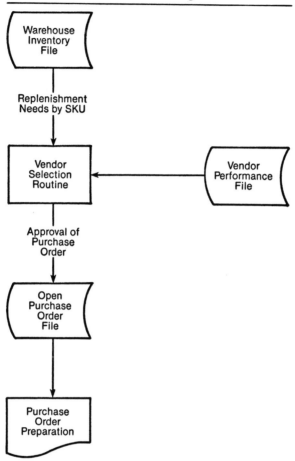

After receipt of the material the SKU file and Vendor Performance File can be updated and the fact of the receipt indicated to Accounts Payable for paying the vendor.

In general, it is wise to use one vendor for a high-volume SKU, negotiating the contract for a long period of time and sending blanket orders to the vendor, with requests for shipment as they occur. Groups of slow-moving items can also be procured in this manner to minimize the vendor negotiating problem.

This is *the* key to getting good service, low cost, and high-quality performance from a vendor.

PRODUCTION SCHEDULING
INTERFACE

A warehouse that is being replenished from a production plant can be replenished through a central scheduling activity, or in a multiwarehousing system through a push system at the plant, which uses inventory records and sales demand to trigger the replenishment needs of the warehouse, or through a pull system in which the warehouse orders material or product directly from the plant.

In central- or plant-controlled systems, the warehouse computer system must supply the status of inventories and the sales demand for each stockkeeping unit on a scheduled basis. The central- or plant-scheduling system then determines the production schedule and the allocation of material to the warehouse.

For a warehouse that is being supplied from a plant on a pull system, the warehouse must determine its needs and then order the material from the plant source and the inventory control system must interface with the production scheduling system. The important points in the computerization of the warehousing system are:

Determine the replenishment lead time required by the plant. This should be accomplished for each SKU.

> Fast-moving or high-volume SKUs should have a short lead time, as the plant should schedule these items frequently and have long production runs.
>
> Slow-moving items should be made once or twice per year to minimize set-up costs at the plant. Material lead time can play a factor, and the ability of the plant to schedule must be taken into consideration.

Determine the replenishment quantity from the plant. Figure 4–9 shows the classical curve for the economic production run. The basis for the economic production run is the set-up cost involved for making a production run of the item. If this set-up cost is high, perhaps because of having to reset machinery, to clean out equipment, to make careful ad-

FIGURE 4–9 Procurement Lot Size and Economic Production Run

Procurement Lot Size

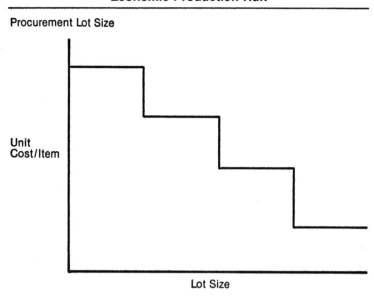

Lot Size

Economic Production Run

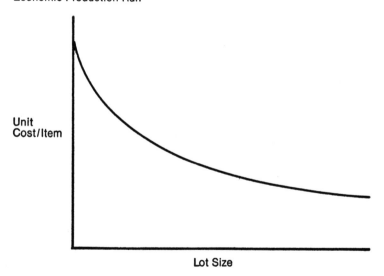

Lot Size

justments, or to add tooling, and the like, then the amount of finished goods made must absorb this set-up cost. An extreme example should illustrate this point. If a Detroit automobile manufacturer spent $50 million to gear up to make a new model and only produced one car, that one car would have to absorb the total cost of setting up the tooling, assembly lines, and so forth. The cost for the first car would then be $50 million plus the material and the labor cost to assemble the first car. If the automobile company made a million cars, however, then each of these cars could absorb its fair share of the "set-up" cost, or $50, plus the costs for material and labor for each car.

The warehouse can then order the required quantities from the plant, recognizing the effect of production lot size on its order quantity and replenishment lead time to maximize the productivity of the plant.

The interface from the warehouse computer system to the plant scheduling system should therefore be considered. The warehouse computer system should be able to trigger those items that have reached the reorder point based on the replenishment lead time for the item and then order the proper quantity from the plant.

INVENTORY MANAGEMENT

This third level of inventory control operations, after inventory status or record keeping and inventory control over stock levels and replenishment, is the management of inventories, which encompasses:

> The proper location of inventories in a distribution system. This is essentially a distribution problem and we will not concern ourselves with this function of inventory management.
>
> The proper inventory levels to minimize procurement, delivery, and inventory carrying costs while providing the proper service levels to meet customer needs in terms of quantity.

Proper inventory levels.   An inventory is maintained to provide a buffer between the production or procurement source and customers or users of the inventory and to provide proper service levels to customers. The costs of carrying an inventory is the cost of the investment in the inventory, and this must be weighed against the potential profit from the sales made out of the inventory.

Let us take a representative inventory of 100 SKUs. Pareto's law shows that about 20 SKUs will account for 80 percent of our sales in units, about 30 SKUs will account for about 15 percent of sales, and 50 SKUs will account for only 5 percent of sales.

The 20 fast-moving items can generally be forecast accurately and demand is generally consistent; these items can also frequently be procured in relatively large quantities. There should therefore be minimum inventories, perhaps an average of 4 weeks or 10 turns of inventory, because of rapid, scheduled replenishments. High service levels close to 100 percent in stock to meet customer orders should be maintained. This means that we will cover 80 percent of our total demand (100 percent service for 80 percent of the demand) and have 8 percent of our total sales in inventory (80 percent of our annual sales turning 10 times for 8 percent of our inventory in stock for fast movers).

In a like manner, we can look at the 30 SKUs that account for 15 percent of the sales volume. We will have to have more inventory, perhaps an average supply of 10 weeks, or 5 turns of inventory in stock, and our service level might be only 90 percent. This means that we will have 3 percent of our annual sales in inventory (15 percent of total sales divided by the 5 turns) and a total service level of 13.5 percent (90 percent service on 15 percent of total sales).

The slow movers will have to be replenished in relatively large quantities because of the economic production quantity for small quantities and the minimum-order quantity for vendor products. We could therefore procure a year's supply of each item, giving an average inventory of 6 months, or 2 turns of inventory for these items. The inventory level will therefore be 2.5 percent of annual sales in inventory (5 percent annual sales divided by 2 turns) but the service level should be close to 100 percent because of the high average inventory giving a service level of 5 percent of total sales (100 percent in stock times the 5 percent of sales accounted for by the slow moving items).

Total service to customers will be 98.5 percent:

Fast movers   100 percent × 80 percent of sales = 80.0 percent service
Medium movers   90 percent × 15 percent of sales = 13.5 percent service
Slow movers   100 percent × 5 percent of sales = _5.0_ percent service
Total   98.5

and our inventory levels will be:

Fast movers   80 percent of sales ÷ 10 turns = 8.0 percent of annual sales
                                                                                      in inventory
Medium movers 15 percent of sales ÷ 5 turns = 3.0 percent of annual sales
                                                                                     in inventory
Slow movers   5 percent of sales ÷ 2 turns = 2.5 percent of annual sales
                                                                                   in inventory
Total   13.5

Thus, 13.5 percent of total sales in inventory is 7 turns or about a 7-week average supply in inventory.

Some companies and institutions will have higher inventories because of longer replenishment lead times or lack of controls, while others will have lower inventories. It is up to the inventory control system to determine the optimum inventory level for a particular inventory application.

Tight controls must be placed on the forecasting, inventory control, replenishing, and procurement of the fast-moving items if inventories are to be minimized and service levels to be maximized.

CHECK SHEET

This chapter has covered the Product Master File, the Inventory File, and the interactive routines of updating the Inventory File from receipts, rewarehousing, and withdrawals. A summary check sheet is shown in Figure 4–10 for the system designer to ensure that the major points are covered for the design of the system.

FIGURE 4–10
Inventory Control Check Sheet

Definition of each stockkeeping unit
  Product categories
  Item-numbering system
  Units of the SKU
  Package quantities of the SKU. Pallets, cartons, innerpacks,
    pieces
  Length, width, and height of the package(s)
  Weight of the package
  Quality control specifications
  Security items
  Storage characteristics
  Hazardous material
  Vendor procurement
  Plant procurement
  Etc.

Product Master File
  Determine necessity or whether the inventory file can be used
  System specifications
  CRT screen layout
  Print-out of catalogs

Inventory File
  File layout
  CRT screen
  Additions, changes, and deletions
    New items
    Changed items
    Receiving routine
    Inspection routine
    Storages
    Rewarehousing
    Allocation to customer orders
    Picking
    Packing
    Inspection
    Withdrawals for damages, obsoletes, etc.
    Shipping
  Inventory status reports
  Inquiry routines

FIGURE 4–10 (continued)

Inventory control
    Pareto curve. SKUs listed in descending order of usage
    Proper units for the Pareto curve
    Identification of fast, medium, and slow movers
    Procurement or production-replenishment lead times
    Procurement-minimum-order quantity
    Reorder points
    Reorder quantities
Interface with the purchasing system or production planning
    system

Inventory management
    Fast movers with minimum inventories and high service levels
    Medium movers with higher inventories and lower service
    levels
    Slow movers with high service levels and high inventory levels

5

Receipts and Inbound Quality Control

"Proper control over receiving gives proper control
over the warehouse."

The mission of a warehouse is to receive, store, pick, prepare,
package, and ship orders for material to customers or users of
the material maintained in the warehouse. Proper receiving
procedures must be incorporated in the function of the warehouse to ensure accurate counts of *and* proper quality of each
item of inbound material. This is important for the fulfillment
of the final mission of the warehouse—to supply the proper
material to the customers or end users.

THE WAREHOUSE AS A BANK

The warehouse must be considered to be a bank that receives
valuable or important merchandise or material that must be
accounted for and securely and carefully kept until withdrawn
by the users of the merchandise or material.

It is therefore necessary to integrate the receiving function
with not only the warehouse inventory and stock location control system, but also with the following:

Purchasing or replenishment system to indicate that the material ordered has been received in the correct quantities and with the proper specifications.

Accounting system to transfer the ownership of the material to the warehouse.

Accounts payable system, if material is purchased from outside vendors or sources, for proof of delivery to allow payment or transfer of funds to the supplier.

These system interfaces must be defined and designed in a computerized warehousing system and will play an important part in the success of using the computer to increase the performance of the warehouse. Common sense dictates, however, that the receiving system must also take into major consideration the physical activities of the receiving and inspection function.

The elements, or subsystems, of receipts control are:

Transfer of "title" from the delivery system

Unloading the material in the warehouse

Checking for quantity of material

Accumulation of the material on the receiving dock and control over it

Preparation of the Receiving Report

Interface with the Purchasing or Production Scheduling System

Inspection and identification of the stockkeeping unit received

Inspection specifications

Inspection accumulation and hold areas

Release of material to the storage function

Identification and count of material released from receiving and inspection to storage

RECEIVING vs. INSPECTION

In some warehouses, receiving and inspection can be combined into one operating function, and the receivers will have the responsibility for not only receiving the material from an outside source but also will have the responsibility for proper identification of the item received and the assurance that what was received meets the specifications for the stockkeeping unit. In other warehouses, this function must be divided into two areas of responsibility, the *receiving* function and the *inspection* function.

1. *Receiving function.* The receivers are only responsible for unloading and moving the material into the warehouse and transferring "title" of the packages or containers to the warehouse. They have the responsibility of counting the containers, whether they be pallets, cartons, or other physical units, and noting whether there is potential damage by inspecting the external appearance of the container. The receivers will then place the material in an inbound accumulation area to await formal inspection.

2. *Inspection function.* The inspection function has the responsibility for the final count of the material received and the assurance that the material is what has been ordered by or for the warehouse.

This division of responsibility between the receiving and the inspection functions is based on the characteristics of individual Stockkeeping Units maintained in the warehouse. Some items require a more accurate count and physical inspection than others. For example, corrugated shipping containers generally do not need to be inspected and counted as rigorously as, say, labels or raw materials for a pharmaceutical warehouse, inbound material from a new vendor or unreliable source, high-cost items, or specialized or highly technical electronic components that must be absolutely correct.

This means that the first order of business will be to identify the quality-control requirements for each stockkeeping unit maintained in the warehouse and then to develop the receiving and inspection system to meet these requirements. Some items can be received and directly transferred to inventory, while others must go through a very rigorous inspection and quality-control procedure prior to being released to storage.

TRANSFER OF "TITLE"
FROM THE DELIVERY SYSTEM

The receiving function has the responsibility for receiving material into the warehouse from an outside source, whether it be a vendor shipment or a shipment from a related manufacturing source.

The key element is that the material is under someone else's control—either trucker, railroad, delivery service, production system, and the like—until it crosses a magic line drawn in the warehouse, where it becomes the property and responsibility of the warehouse and the "title" to the material transfers to the warehouse. (In using the word "title," we are not using the legalistic definition of the term, but rather the connotation of physical possession or placement of the material. There are many warehouses where the "legal" title of material is kept in the hands of third parties).

The receivers in a system that receives materials by common carriers—truckers, the U.S. Postal Service, or the many other companies that provide transportation services—are responsible for checking the number of cartons or containers that have been received and ensuring that the receipt is proper. Quite frequently, this means checking that the material has been properly ordered by or for the warehouse.

Refusal of deliveries. In some retail warehouses, vendors will ship material that has not been ordered by or for the warehouse. These vendors hope that with the proof of receipt, the company will pay for the merchandise. It is therefore necessary to specify to the receiving function what constitutes the proof that the material has been ordered for the warehouse and that it should be received and, conversely, what inbound shipments should be rejected and returned to the shipper.

This proof is generally a valid Purchase Order Number that has been issued by the company or institution. In a computerized system the receiver can make a CRT check against the Open Purchase Order File.

Signing the Bill of Lading or Manifest. The receivers have the responsibility for signing the inbound transportation document to indicate that the proper number of containers has been received, noting any possible damages that might be evident from the condition of the container. For transfers of material from one company-owned facility to another, it can be assumed that the transfer has been authorized and the material is of the proper quality. However, the material should be inspected for proper identification, quantity, and quality, if there is *any* possibility of mistaken identity, quantity, or quality of the inbound material. There could be a need to check the production order, item specification, or other ordering documents.

UNLOADING

Tailgate deliveries. The responsibility for unloading common carrier deliveries is generally the responsibility of the trucker, unless the items are large and require mechanized equipment. The warehouse must unload some shipments if special rates have been negotiated for consignee unloading. The receiver can therefore have the responsibility to supply the trucker with any needed equipment and then ensure that proper counts are made of the containers received.

Unloading by warehouse personnel. For rail cars, company-owned trucks, or when the negotiated rate with the common carrier does not include unloading, it is the responsibility of the warehouse to unload the inbound vehicle. The receiving function here has the responsibility to get the proper equipment and manpower to do the physical unloading of the material and to make a proper count of the containers received, noting and setting aside any containers that have been tampered with or have been damaged.

The carrier documents must then be signed by the receiver to indicate that the proper quantity of containers has been received, with a notation of any over, short, or damaged containers. These documents form the basis for legal completion of (or exceptions to) the delivery transaction.

Proper receiving facilities. The receiving area of the warehouse should be controlled to maintain security of the material in the warehouse. This means that ingress and egress should be limited to those truckers or visitors that have the authority to enter the facility. Doorways and docks should be designed to minimize the ability of outsiders to enter the facility. Guard stations should be incorporated into the design to keep intruders out. Separate trucker washroom facilities and a pay telephone are desirable for larger warehouses.

The truck docks and unloading facilities should be well lit and air conditioned, as appropriate to the material being handled and to provide good working conditions for the warehouse personnel.

Painted lines on the floor and signs should designate areas that carrier personnel can work. A barrier, either physical or painted lines, should separate the dock from the warehouse work and storage areas.

The physical equipment on the dock—conveyors, mobile equipment, and racks and other storage equipment—should be tailored to the type of material received. Computer-controlled equipment such as automatically guided vehicle systems, conveyor-diversion systems, automatic storage/retrieval systems, automatic palletizers and depalletizers, and optical scanning or bar-code-reading systems should be incorporated into the receiving area in a computer-controlled warehousing system.

Accumulation areas in receiving.   Accumulation areas on the receiving docks should be used to accumulate received material prior to being put away or transferred to inspection. These areas are necessary, as it is a well-known law of Murphy that all inbound trucks will arrive at the receiving dock at the same time. The material must therefore be received and unloaded to the accumulation areas rather than going directly into storage or to the inspection station.

These accumulation areas can be painted locations on the floor of the receiving dock or pallet racks or shelving. A random location and control system can be used if there are a large number of receipts, or a significant lead time between the receipt and storage or inspection of the material.

PREPARATION OF THE
RECEIVING REPORT

The Receiving Report can be prepared by the receiver if there is no doubt as to the proper quality and quantity of the receipt and there is no indication of damage to the material. This Receiving Report can be prepared manually and then entered into the computer, or the receiving information can be directly entered by CRT.

A typical Receiving Report is shown on Figure 5-1a. The

FIGURE 5-1a Typical Receiving Report

Time	Carrier	Reference Number	Item Number	Description	Quantity	Container or Pack	Weight	Notes O, S, & D	Receiver
RECEIVING REPORT						SHIFT	X	DATE	XX/XX/XX
XXXX	XXX	XXXXX	XXXXX	XXXXXXX	XXXXX	XXX	XXX	XXXXXXXXXXX	XXXX

FIGURE 5-1b CRT Screen Receiving Format

RECEIVING REPORT

Date	XX/XX/XX		Time	XXXX		Receiver	XXXX

Carrier   XXX   B/L No.   XXXXX
                                   Manifest No.   XXXXX
                                   Car No.   XXXXX

Purchase Order No.   XXXXX   Vendor   XXXXX

Item No.	Description	Quantity	Package	Weight	Notes
XXXXX	XXXXXXX	XXXXX	XXX	XXX	XXXXX

Receiving Report will have the date, the time, the carrier, the Purchase Order Number, Bill of Lading or Manifest Number, the item number, a short description if necessary, the number of containers, and perhaps the total or individual weight of the containers received.

The receiving function can also prepare the Receiving Report using the computer. Here the pertinent information is entered into a CRT at the dock and a printout can be made, if appropriate. An illustrative CRT screen is shown on Figure 5-1b.

INTERFACE WITH THE OPEN PURCHASE ORDER FILE OR PRODUCTION SCHEDULING FILE

A CRT on the receiving dock will allow direct inquiry by the receivers to the Open Purchase Order or Scheduled Production Shipments File for the assurance that the inbound shipment is a valid shipment. This provides the receiver with the authority to receive the inbound shipment.

The CRT can also show the pertinent information on the Purchase Order, the item ordered, the package quantity of the item, and the number of cartons or containers to be received. This assists the receiver in ensuring that the proper material is being received and in the proper quantities.

Figure 5-2 shows the schematic representation of the CRT interfaces with the Purchase Order File. The operations required are:

> Entry of the Purchase Order Number
>
> Entry of the vendor in the event that there is no Purchase Order designation on the shipment to determine whether there is an open PO for this material. Once the vendor number is known, the receiver can check the Open Purchase Order File for the types of material and find the Purchase Order Number if there is one.
>
> The complete Purchase Order can appear on the screen. This will allow the receiver to know the items and the quantities

FIGURE 5-2 Receiving CRT Interface with Purchase Order or Production Requisition System

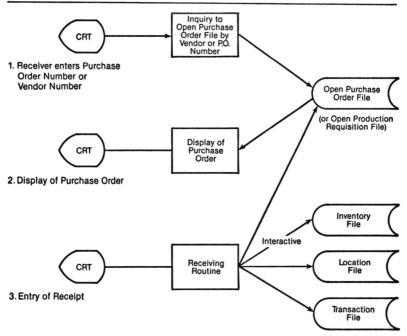

that have been ordered. The receiver can then receive the material, unload it, and place it in the proper accumulation area or put the material directly in storage.

The receiver can then indicate via the CRT that the warehouse has received the actual quantities that were designated on the Purchase Order or the actual quantities received. Overages, shorts, and damaged material can also be entered.

Blind receiving. In a blind receiving system, the receiver can call up the Purchase Order to find the items that have been ordered but the quantities will *not* appear (be blind) on the screen. This forces the receiver to enter the actual quantities received, which are then compared by the computer with the correct quantities. This procedure is used when it is necessary to eliminate, or attempt to eliminate, collusion between the receiver, trucker, and/or vendor. In either event, the receiver can enter the received quantities of material for the shipment.

A transaction report can also be made to a computer Transaction File, showing the date, item, package quantity, and quantity of packages that have been received, including the receiver's badge number or initials. This transaction report can be used for audit trails and productivity reporting for the receiving function.

The inventory and location files can also be updated at this time to indicate that the material has been received—but not inspected or put into storage.

INSPECTION AND IDENTIFICATION OF INBOUND MATERIAL

All material received in the warehouse must be identified. This means inspecting the material to be sure that it is what has been ordered or needed by the warehouse and that the proper warehouse identification number is assigned to it.

Identification of the item is very important in maintenance or raw material warehouses where there can be technological differences that are very important to the end user. The material cannot be considered for picking to customer orders until the warehouse is assured that the item is the item that the customer or user wants.

Ideally, the vendor or production source should be responsible for the proper identification of each inbound container. It will not be long before bar codes or optical characters will be standard on all containers so that the identification will be machine readable. At this time, however, the use of bar codes or optical character-recognition equipment should be considered as a part of the Receiving-Inspection function. Labels can be printed or the container can be printed with the identification number and quantity so that future movement transactions can be machine read and entered directly into the computer. The preparation of labels or identification can be accomplished at the receiving dock or in the quality-control inspection area.

Material returns from end users or customers must be handled by some warehouses. Here, the material must be inspected for the proper identification, quality, and quantity, and a decision must be made to return the material to storage for other customers or to make other disposition of the material. Quite frequently, this will occur in another, separate, area of the warehouse. Returns can be controlled by the computer system in a manner similar to any receipt of the warehouse, but could have additional reporting requirements to marketing and production control.

QUALITY CONTROL INSPECTIONS

All material entering a warehouse must be inspected to ensure that it is of the proper quality. The degree of quality inspection varies from:

Cursory inspection.   This is for material that will not have a major effect on the customer or end user of the material if it is incorrect. There is little chance of economic losses to the company, or institution, if the material is incorrect. Items such as corrugated containers, dunnage, and so on, are examples of the type of items that can be received and inspected at the receiving dock and put directly into storage.

Receiver's inspection and tally.   For material that is received from other company-owned facilities or known reliable vendors that have no history of quality or quantity problems, the receiver's visual inspection, identification of the item, and count of the receipts can be considered sufficient for quality control purposes.

Random inspections by quality control.   Some items will require an inspection by a designated quality control person in the warehouse. This person will ensure that the item is what the warehouse has ordered, take an accurate count of the quantity, and make a random inspection that the material meets the specifications for the warehouse.

Detailed inspection by quality control. There are some items that will require a higher level of inspection to ensure that the items are 100 percent correct.

Murphy's Law states that if something can go wrong it will. The procurement or production of material is no exception. The reason for quality control inspections at, or after, receipt of goods is to ensure that only the proper quality and quantity of material is put into storage for future withdrawal by customers or end users. These types of items should therefore be inspected very rigorously based on the specifications for the item that have been developed by the user, purchasing, or engineering.

Technical inspections. These items must be physically inspected, measured, or tested to determine whether they are up to the specifications required for the item. These items can be parts for production, parts for maintenance equipment, or any items that are to be sold or used for very stringent customer or user requirements.

The specifications for the Stockkeeping Unit must be available for the inspector and can be drawings or specification sheets in files, on microfiche, or on a CRT display of the drawings, specifications, and test and inspection procedures.

A CRT at the inspection station can provide the information necessary for the inspection and quality control functions. This display is shown on Figure 5-3, Quality Control Specifications for Stockkeeping Units, and will include:

Stockkeeping unit number

The item description

The specifications for the item

The testing procedure that must be used for the item

INSPECTION AREAS
AND ACCUMULATION AREAS

For some warehouses, there will be defined lined or caged areas between the receiving dock and the inspection area and

FIGURE 5–3 Qualilty Control Specifications for Stockkeeping Units

CRT SCREEN FOR INSPECTION

SKU Number   XXXXX

SKU Description   XXXXXXXXXX

                 XXX XXX XXX

Specification:		Test Procedure:	
1.	XXXXX	1.	XXXX
2.	XXXXX	2.	XXXX
3.	XXXXX	3.	XXXX
4.	XXXXX	4.	XXXX
5.	XXXXX	5.	XXXX

Sample or full inspection   XXXXX

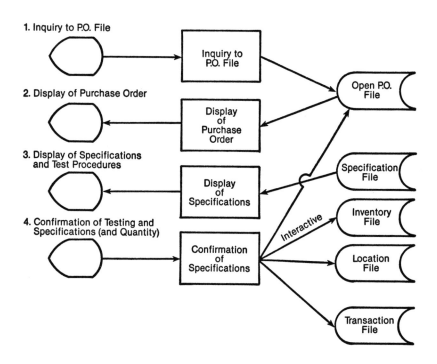

1. Inquiry to P.O. File
2. Display of Purchase Order
3. Display of Specifications and Test Procedures
4. Confirmation of Testing and Specifications (and Quantity)

Inquiry to P.O. File

Display of Purchase Order

Display of Specifications

Confirmation of Specifications

Open P.O. File

Specification File

Inventory File

Location File

Transaction File

Interactive

85

between the inspection area and the storage area to ensure that no material will be put into storage until the material is properly inspected. This type of control should be considered in any warehouse because of the potential economic loss to the company if material finds its way into storage that is not of proper quality and a legal action could result if the material is shipped to a customer.

Accumulation areas for inbound material for inspection can be painted lines on the warehouse floor for pallets or carts, shelving, racks, or automated storage/retrieval systems. The material is placed in the accumulation area by the receiving function. The system can be a random location system with a locator system that allows the inspection group to find the product once they are ready to inspect it. Inbound material can be color coded for each day to provide a visual indicator of the backlog behind the inspectors.

In a like manner, the output of the inspection or quality control function can be accumulated prior to transfer to the storage areas.

INTERFACE BETWEEN
THE INSPECTION OR QUALITY CONTROL
STATION AND THE COMPUTER

This is shown on Figure 5-3 and allows the quality control inspector to enter the results of the inspection into the computer Inventory File, Open Purchase Order File, and Transaction File.

IDENTIFICATION
OF STOCKKEEPING UNITS

The proper and correct identification of the containers—pallets, cases, and so forth—must be accomplished in the receiving-inspection function. The physical units should be marked with the warehouse identification number and in some cases with the number of pieces or units that are in the package.

STORAGE OF MATERIAL

The material can now be put into storage. As described in Chapter 6 on stock location, the location of material can be controlled by the computer or by the storers in the warehouse. If the material is controlled by the computer, the stock location can be determined by the receiver or inspector and placed on the container for use by the storer. This identification of the item, the quantity, and the location can be accomplished by:

> Location tickets prepared by a printer in the receiving or inspection station
> Manually prepared location tickets

In either event, the material must be identified and physically marked with the necessary information prior to being moved from the receiving dock or the inspection station to storage.

Some material can be transferred directly to the outbound shipping locations instead of going into storage. This occurs in master distribution warehouses that transship material received from outside sources to regional depots. In this case, the material, after inspection, will be allocated to end users and transferred to an outbound shipping location. The receipt, therefore, triggers the Open Order File to transfer the receipt directly to an outbound shipment.

In a like manner, material received that is on back order can bypass the storage function and be directly assigned to an outbound order and transferred to the shipping dock after proper identification of the customer or end user and the preparation of shipping labels and documents.

These cross-dock transfers should be designed into the system, if relevant, by the computer system receiving the material and then allocating it directly to an outbound shipment.

CHECK SHEET FOR RECEIVING
AND INBOUND QUALITY CONTROL

In order to computerize the receiving operations of a warehouse, the design characteristics must be determined for the physical activities of the function, the proper receiving and inspection equipments determined, and then the total system integrated with the computer.

A check sheet is shown on Figure 5-4 that outlines the major factors that must be considered.

FIGURE 5-4
Check Sheet for Receiving
and Inbound Quality Control

Receiving design factors
  Receipts per day
  Line items per day
  Inbound schedule of deliveries
  Mode of inbound receipt
    Common carriers
      Rail
      Truck
      UPS
      USPS
  Own truck fleet or contract carriage
  Direct from production or assembly operations

Type of container
  Truck or container loads
  Pallets
  Drums or other unit loads
  Cartons
  Bags
  Small items

Stockkeeping unit list showing confidence in quality and quantity of inbound receipts
  Cursory inspection is OK
  More detailed count by receiver but quality is OK
  Random inspection for count, identification, and quality
  100 percent inspection
  Highly detailed quality control inspection

Physical layout and spatial arrangement of receiving area
  Docks
  Ingress and egress areas
  Accumulation areas
  Inspection areas

FIGURE 5–4 (continued)

Trucker facilities
Lighting and air conditioning

Design considerations
Automated equipment for
Unloading
Sorting
Conveying and diverting
Counting
Application of identification codes
Palletization and depalletization

Computer interfaces
Receiving report
Open purchase order or production scheduling file
Inventory File
Specifications File
Transaction File

6

Stock Location
and Space Utilization

"A Place for Everything and Everything in Its Place"

Warehouse space costs money. Warehousing space is an investment in the area used for storing and processing inventories and, like any asset, space usage must be controlled. The more material that can be stored in a given space, the better. However, the effect of congestion must be considered as to its effect on labor costs. If the warehouse is too crowded, labor will be used to move things about, to search for the items wanted, and to correct errors that are made because of not having a location for every item and having every item in its proper place.

In this chapter, we will discuss the development of a computerized stock-location system that will contain the location of all of the items in the inventory, ensure an accurate inventory count, and provide control information for the utilization of the space assigned to the warehouse operation.

ELEMENTS OF STOCK LOCATION
AND SPACE UTILIZATION

The elements of a stock-location and space-utilization computer-control system are:

The Warehouse Location Matrix. This is a map of the warehouse showing every storage location and every type of storage cell. It will also contain the storage capacity of each storage cell in cubic measurements (cubic inches or feet or the metric system).

The updating of the Stock Location Matrix File with:

Receipts

Rewarehousing activities

Allocation of the stock to orders by location

The picking of material from the locations to replenish a forward picking line

The picking of customer orders

The control of the location system to ensure accuracy by having cycle counts or physical inventories.

The preparation of reports on space utilization for total warehouse control, space assigned to products, and, if appropriate, space assigned to customers.

The use of the Warehouse Location Matrix for determining the *proper picking paths* and the *development of standard travel times*.

WAREHOUSE LAYOUT

The first step in the development of a warehouse location system is to define the warehouse aisle and storage arrangement. Figure 6–1 is a typical warehouse showing the locations of receiving, inspection, bulk pallet storage, pallet rack storage, shelving, bins, forward pick lines, packing, and shipping. This "map" of the warehouse should be prepared utilizing the layout of the facility and based on the warehousing system for receiving, inspection, storage, picking, packing, and shipping. Of course, other areas for returned goods, kitting operations, and semi-production functions should be included on the layout.

FIGURE 6-1 Warehouse Layout

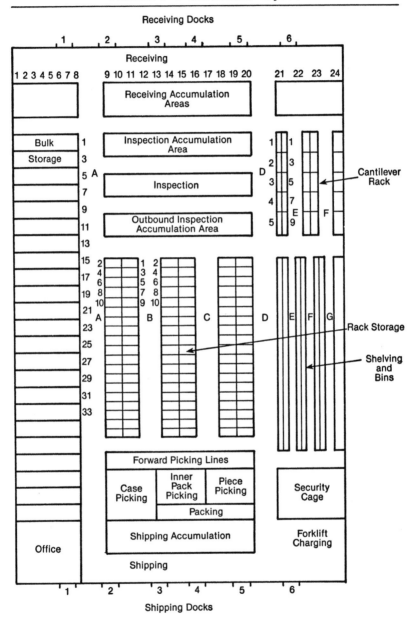

The aisle dimensions should be determined, as well as the dimensions of each of the storage cells used.

It is a rule of good warehousing that every item or SKU in a warehouse must be readily accessible to the warehouse employee. This eliminates searching and the time necessary to move items out of the way to find the item that is being sought.

STORAGE CELLS

A storage cell defines the area in a warehouse where inventory can be stored. Figure 6–2 shows the types of cells that are generally encountered in warehouse operations.

Bulk storage of pallets. Pallets can be stacked one on top of each other in deep rows of storage. This is bulk storage for pallets. The dimensions of the cell for storage of inventory of an SKU is the front dimension or width; the depth of storage, depending on how many pallets can be stored; and the height of storage, or how many pallets can be stacked one on top of another.

Dimensions of a bulk storage cell are dependent upon the pallet size being used. For a 40-inch-wide by 48-inch-deep pallet the dimensions of the cell might be 43 inches wide (which allows for a 3-inch clearance between the pallets) and multiples of 4 feet deep, depending on the number of pallets that could be stored in the cell.

(A 3-inch-wide painted line is usually used to define the storage cell for bulk storage of pallets.)

Pallet racks. For some items, pallets cannot be stacked one on top of another because of the potential crushing of the material on the pallet. For this type of pallet load, the use of drive-through pallet racks for high-volume items can be used to get the advantage of bulk storage. Here, the forklift truck will drive into the rack to place the pallet on the floor or on lips that extend from the rack uprights for holding the pallet.

FIGURE 6–2 Storage Cells

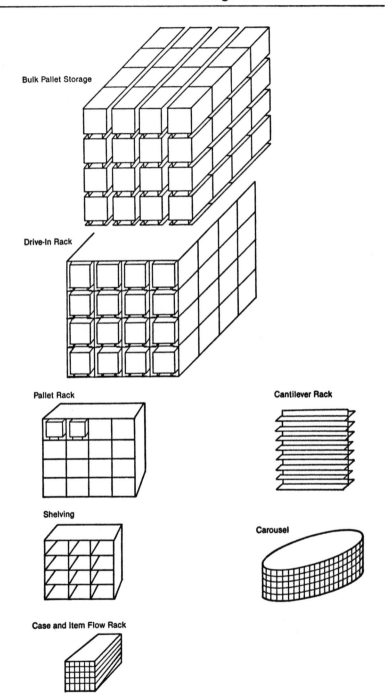

Bulk Pallet Storage

Drive-In Rack

Pallet Rack

Cantilever Rack

Shelving

Carousel

Case and Item Flow Rack

94

Pallet racks can also be one deep for storage of single pallets for ease in getting to the pallet when needed.

The sizing and dimensioning of the pallet rack, either drive-through or singulated, is dependent on the pallet dimensions and the rack supports, and, the depth of storage of pallets in a pallet drive-through rack.

Cantilever rack. Cantilever racks hold long, narrow items, such as pipe, rugs, and the like. The dimensions necessary here are the length of the rack, the width, and the height of each opening, allowing for clearances.

Shelving. Shelving is used to store cartons, inner packs, or pieces of an SKU and depends on the characteristics of the package that is to be stored. Standard shelving is 3 to 6 feet long by $1\frac{1}{2}$ to 2 feet deep (to allow ease in reaching in to get the item by the picker), and 6 to 8 feet high. The dimensions needed are the depth of the storage cell, the width of the shelf that is to be assigned to the items in inventory, and the height of the shelf. In a typical example of shelved items, the cell under consideration might be 1 foot wide, 1 foot high, and $1\frac{1}{2}$ feet deep, as might be found in a form-supply warehouse, a pharmaceutical warehouse, or a retail distribution warehouse for consumer items.

The three dimensions of the storage cell will provide the cube of the cell. This will be stored in the computer warehouse Location Matrix File.

Bin sections. Many warehouses have very small items that are contained in various sized bins. Here the individual bin dimensions must be obtained, the width of front, the depth, and the usable height of the bin. In bins with subdivisions, each of the subdivisions should be considered as a storage cell, and the dimensions obtained.

Carousel bins. These are bin or shelving sections that can rotate either horizontally or vertically, which allow the picker to remain stationary while the material or picking section moves to the picker. The dimensions of width, depth, and height should be determined.

Forward case or item-picking flow racks. These are used in many warehouses to contain SKUs in a small area to minimize picker travel time. They are generally deep storage (5 to 20 feet), and must be replenished from the rear, while the picker takes the item from the front. The dimensions of the flow rack cells are based on the dimensions of the package unit that will be placed in it for height and width; the length is based on the flow rack dimensions.

Push-through shelving with open backs can also be effectively used as flow racks, being replenished from the rear and picked from the front.

Accumulation areas. Accumulation areas must be used in warehouses to take care of peak receiving, inspection, order picking, and shipping volumes. These are work-in-process storage cells and can also be defined, not so much for space utilization purposes, but for operating purposes. They should be sized and shown on the warehouse Location Matrix File, for determining travel distances for standards development, and for proper location and control of stock as it moves through the warehouse. The locations of receiving, shipping, and any other areas in the warehouse must be defined on the location matrix.

WAREHOUSE LOCATION
MATRIX FILE

From the warehouse layout and the definition of each of the storage cells, a location matrix for the warehouse can be laid out, much as a street map of a city can be developed. The aisles and cross-aisles must be defined, usually by an alphabetical code, for example, Aisle A, B, C, and so forth. The storage cells can then be defined by numerals. For singular rack section, shelving sections, or flow rack and bin sections, the main floor spot of the rack can be designated, but the levels or tiers must also be defined. This is analogous to an apartment building in the city, where the floor will define the tier that the apartment is on. And the final step will be to define subtiers as necessary. For example, on a 3-foot-wide shelf, three SKUs might be stored; these would be numbered 1, 2, and 3.

For bin sections with subdivisions, this could lead to a fifth level of identification: namely, aisle, bin section, level in the bin section, subtier, and subdivisions in the bin.

Figure 6–3 shows the Location Matrix File in the computer indicating:

Aisle   The "street" that the cell is on
Spot   The address on the street of the storage cell
Tier   The level, or height, that the cell is on
Subtier   The apartment number of the cell
Sub-subtier The subdivision of the cell

This matrix, therefore, will define each cell in the warehouse as to location and type of storage. Special storage areas such as refrigerated or hazardous material storage should be defined in the matrix.

The next step is to determine the dimensions of each of the cells in terms of width of the front of the cell, the depth of the cell, and the usable height of the cell. These dimensions should be obtained to the nearest $\frac{1}{8}$ inch. The computer can then compute the cube for each of the cells.

A map of the warehouse is then in the computer file. This "map" can be modified by warehouse personnel as changes are made or new storage equipment is installed. An updating procedure must be developed to keep the computer Location Matrix File in exactly the same configuration as the actual warehouse.

The computer can print out the Location Matrix File showing each of the cells and the available cube in each cell. This can be sorted by type of cell and the total cubic capacity for each type of storage cell computed, and, of course, the total storage capacity of the warehouse can be determined. Aisles and work areas are not in the location matrix. If the

FIGURE 6-3 Warehouse Location Matrix and Screen Format

FILE FORMAT FOR WAREHOUSE LOCATION MATRIX

Aisle	Spot	Tier	Subtier	Sub-Subtier	Width	Length	Height	Cube	Type	SKU	Quan.	Cube/Pack	Total Cube	Percent Utilization
XX	XX	XX	XX	XX	XX.X	XX.X	XX.X	XXXX.X	XX	XXXXX	XXX	XXX.X	XXXX.X	XX.X

WAREHOUSE LOCATION MATRIX SCREEN

Aisle   XX   Type XX
Spot   XX
Tier   XX
Subtier   XX
Sub-Subtier   XX
Length XX.X   Width XX.X   Height XX.X   Cube XXXX.X
SKU   XXXXX
Pack   XXXXX

Cube per Pack XX.X   Total Cube   XXXX.X
                                      Cube Utilization   XX.X

total cubic feet of space in the warehouse is calculated, the available storage space can be expressed as a percent of the total cubic feet available.

LOADING THE LOCATION
MATRIX FILE

Once the Location Matrix File has been defined and loaded into the computer, the next step will be to load the inventory into the file. This is accomplished by determining what SKU is in each storage cell, the package or container, and the number of packages that are in the storage cell.

Then, the Product Master or Inventory File is consulted to determine the length, width, and height of the SKU package that is in the storage cell. This could be expressed in pallets, cases, inner-packs, or individual pieces of the item.

This information is then loaded into the storage cells of the location matrix (Figure 6–3). The SKU number has been defined; the length, width, and height of the item has been placed in the proper cell; and the quantity of the particular package for the SKU in the cell is quantified.

The computer will then multiply the number of SKU packages by the cube of the package to show the *cube that has been used in the storage cell.*

From this, a space utilization percentage can be calculated by the computer to indicate the percent of space available for storage that has been used by the material in the cell.

The database for the Location Matrix File is therefore the map of the warehouse that shows the aisle, spot, tier, and sub- or sub-subtier in the facility.

We will now follow the path of material through the warehouse and see the effects on the warehouse Location Matrix File.

RECEIVING

The stock location system can include the receiving accumulation area. As material is received, the stock can be placed in a location in this receiving accumulation area and the computer notified of this location. As the material is transferred to inspection, or to storage, this file will be reduced.

INSPECTION
AND QUALITY CONTROL

The move of material to the Inspection and Quality Control accumulation area can be reported.

As material is inspected for both quantity and quality, the computer will be notified of the results of the inspection. Notification can also be made when the material is moved from inspection and is put into storage.

RANDOM vs. DESIGNATED STORAGE

There are two methods of storing. One is on a *random basis* where material can be placed in any available storage cell that can contain the particular quantity and characteristics of the package. Controls must of course be established over the locations of each stockkeeping unit so as to be able to find the item when needed. Reserve inventories and pallet inventories are generally maintained in random storage locations, as random storage systems have the effect of maximizing cube utilization.

Forward picking lines, shelving, bin sections, and cantilever rack sections generally have *designated* storage cells. In a designated storage system, every SKU is assigned a "home" and inventory of the SKU is kept in that designated cell. This makes it easier for the picker to find the item and allows a standard path for picking customer orders.

STORING

In a designated storage system, the computer can designate where the material is to be put by searching for the location assigned to the SKU and conveying this information to the storer.

Figure 6-3 shows a CRT screen layout for the Location Matrix File that shows the SKU and the locations that the material is in. The storer can refer to this screen to determine the location for the designated storage items.

For a random storage system, two methods are available for storing product.

Storer controlled. The storer will find a location that is suitable for the quantity of the SKU being stored and will place the material into the cell and notify the computer of the SKU number, the quantity, the date, and badge number or initials.

The computer will then enter this data into the Location Matrix File and also (because of the interactivity between the Inventory File and the Location Matrix File) into the Inventory File.

Computer controlled. In this situation, the storer will request a location for storage from the computer by providing the computer with the SKU, the package unit, and the number of packages. The computer will compute the cube required, search for the storage spots available (considering any special requirement of the SKU for special types of storage), find a location, and then inform the storer of the proper cell to place the material.

The storer will then place the material into the storage location and confirm the transaction with the computer, giving badge number or initials.

REWAREHOUSING

A major objective for many warehouses is to maximize the utilization of cube. A random reserve storage system, where any SKU can be stored in any location, allows this to be accomplished. As the material in the random storage cell is used, either for customer orders or for replenishment to a forward pick line, the inventory in the cell will be depleted and the space used will be reduced.

As storage cells are of different cubic capacities, those cells with poor utilization of cube can be identified and the material can be taken from a "large" cell and moved to a smaller cell where the cube can be more effectively used.

There are two methods for rewarehousing. These are:

1. *Storer controlled.* The storer will search for cells that have low utilization of capacity, note the cube requirements, and then search for a smaller cell that will contain those requirements. The storer will move the material from the first cell to the second cell and notify the computer of the move.

(It should be noted that this can create problems if the computer has allocated the inventory in the cell to a customer's order. Protection should be provided so that the rewarehousing cannot be accomplished if the material in the cell has been allocated to a customer's order.)

2. *Computer controlled.* The storer can have the computer do the rewarehousing routine. The computer will search the warehouse location matrix for cells that have low space utilization. As these are found, the computer can search for empty cells that will contain the cube necessary for the SKU to be moved.

The computer can then notify the storer of the moves to be made. Once they have been made, the computer will be notified by the storer that the transactions have been completed.

ALLOCATION OF MATERIAL
TO CUSTOMER ORDERS

As orders are received, as described in Chapter 3, inventory should be allocated to the customer order. In a like manner, the inventory *in a location* can also be allocated to a customer order. This allows the determination of the standard time for picking the order, the proper picking path when the order is scheduled, the scheduling assignments for group or zone picking; it also forces the inventory to remain in the location until it is picked.

With a designated storage system, of course, such as in forward picking lines, this is not a problem.

REPLENISHMENT OF
FORWARD PICKING LINES

If replenishment of forward picking lines is a part of the warehousing operations, the replenishment can be accomplished in a similar manner to rewarehousing.

1. *Replenisher controlled.* The replenisher will walk the forward pick line and determine those items that need replenishing and the quantities. The replenisher will then pick those items from storage and place them in the pick line and will confirm the transactions with the computer.

2. *Computer controlled.* In a computer-controlled replenishment system, the computer will keep track of the inventory in the forward picking line. When the quantity in the pick line reaches a "reorder point," as material is removed or scheduled from the pick line, the computer will trigger a replenishment order to the replenisher.

The replenisher will then withdraw the inventory from the reserve storage cell and place it in the proper forward picking line spot. The replenisher will then confirm that the transaction was accomplished.

PICKING CUSTOMER ORDERS

The computer will designate the proper location that the material should be picked for a customer order on the picking document. As the material is picked, the computer must be notified that the material has been withdrawn from inventory and the location. This can be accomplished:

As the material is picked.   The picker can notify the computer that the pick was made by key entry into a CRT or as the material passes a scanning system (on a conveyor). The computer can then reduce the inventory.

After the materials have been inspected.   This can be keyed in as the inspector confirms the proper SKU and quantity at an inspection station, or data scanned during or after the inspection process.

At shipping.   This can be done via a CRT or data scan equipment, either prior to loading or after loading.

This confirmation of the picking transaction must be accomplished *after* the picking operation has been completed to ensure that the picker has picked the right SKU in the right quantity from the correct location.

This completes the stock location cycle for material in inventory.

INSPECTION, PACKING, AND SHIPPING LOCATION SYSTEMS

In some warehousing systems, the picked material can be stored in an accumulation area, usually random, awaiting final inspection. The material now assigned to a customer order can be controlled by the computer, both inbound from storage and outbound to packing, shipping accumulation, or the final shipping operation.

WAREHOUSE LOCATION CRT SCREEN

An illustrative screen for a warehouse Location Matrix File is shown on Figure 6-3. This screen shows:

The location by aisle, spot, tier, subtier, or sub-subtier

The SKU in the location

The SKU package in the location

The quantity of the SKU package in the cell

The cube of the material

The percent utilization of the storage cell

And can be modified to show:

The date of storage and person identification

The date of cycle counts and person identification

This screen should allow for updating by responsible warehouse personnel and should be able to be scrolled rapidly to allow for searching for misused cells.

CYCLE COUNTS OR PHYSICAL INVENTORIES

The computer inventory must exactly match the physical inventory in the warehouse.

The accuracy of the inventory will be dependent on the system for storing, rewarehousing, and withdrawing inventory from the storage system. In a man-controlled system, errors will be made if the storers are not disciplined. These errors are caused by transposing numbers for the SKU identification or location, putting the material in the wrong location, withdrawing material from the wrong location, and so on.

The key factor is to have storers who are strongly motivated to do things accurately.

Audits must be made of the inventory to keep the storers and pickers honest. These can be physical inventories taken on a scheduled basis. A physical inventory usually implies a total inventory check done for financial accounting purposes, either once or twice a year. This is not enough for most applications, as errors will compound over time.

A *cycle* count system should be established to ensure the accuracy of the inventory in the computer system. This can be accomplished by having several items or locations checked each day so that corrections and discipline can be done frequently.

In a cycle count system, or for taking physical inventory, the audit can be accomplished either by SKU or by location.

By SKU.   The inventory file is printed out by SKU with locations. This shows the locations of all the material in the warehouse for an SKU. The auditor or checker will go to each of the locations and check that the SKU and quantity are correct.

By location.   Here the Location Matrix File is printed out by location and the auditor goes from location to location checking that the SKU number and quantity are correct.

Corrections are made on the printout and transferred to the Inventory File and Location Matrix File. It is wise to include the date of the cycle count or physical inventory and the person that did the check, using initials or time card number. This allows an audit trail of checks in the warehouse.

The computer inventory and Location Matrix File should be virtually error-free once the people and the system have been working for a time. Errors should be identified and corrected by the cycle count or physical inventory procedure and the responsible warehouse employee notified of the results.

SPACE UTILIZATION REPORTS

The space utilization routine can produce reports from the warehouse Location Matrix File that show space utilized by:

Sub-subtier

Subtier

Tier

Spot

Aisle

Total warehouse

with the space utilized and percent utilization for each type of storage, or for the total warehouse.

With proper programming, the report can be by product class for determining warehouse space used and the costs allocated.

For public warehouses, which store product for their customers, the customer identification can be tied in with the SKU number to give a report by customer, showing the cube allocated and the cube used for each customer.

MULTI-ITEMS
IN A STORAGE CELL

This should not occur. Only one SKU should be in a storage cell. There are situations, however, where because of operational necessity two (or more) SKUs are placed in the same cell. If this must occur, the warehouse Location Matrix File must be designed to allow more than one SKU in the cell. Here, programming must account for the multiplicity of SKUs, the different cubes of the SKUs, and the total cube for each SKU. The computer must then have the capability to add the various SKU cubes together to get a total cube in the cell, and then compute the percent utilization of space in the total cell.

LOCATION MATRIX
AND STANDARDS

The warehouse location matrix will define each location in the warehouse on an x–y axis so that travel distances can be determined by the computer. These travel distances will be used to determine standard travel times for warehouse operations, as discussed in Chapter 7. An illustration of this x–y matrix of a warehouse is shown on Figure 6–4.

This shows the travel distances (in feet) involved from:

	X = Horizontal Distance	Y = Vertical Distance	Total Distance
Receiving Dock 2 to Inspection Accumulation Area 14	70	84	154

FIGURE 6-4 Warehouse Location Matrix—Dimensioned

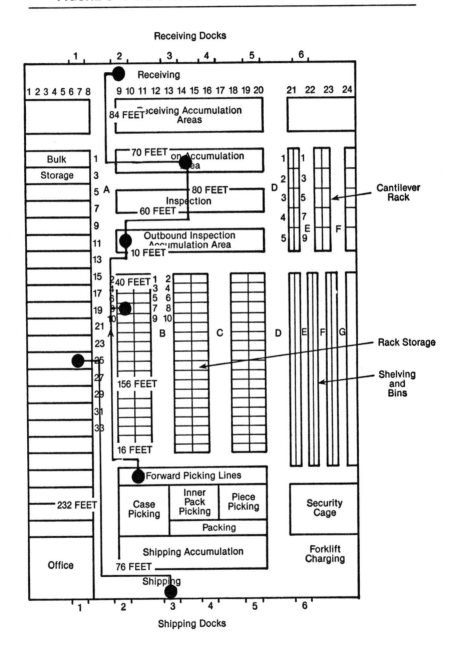

	$X = Horizontal$ *Distance*	$Y = Vertical$ *Distance*	*Total* *Distance*
Inspection Accumulation Area 14 to Outbound Inspection Accumulation Area 9	60	80	140
Outbound Inspection Accumulation 9 to Storage Location A-8	10	40	50
Storage Location A-8 to Forward Case Picking Line	16	156	172
Storage Location A-25 to Shipping Dock 3	76	232	308

As we shall see this will be important in the development of computer-prepared standards and productivity reports.

STOCK LOCATION AND SPACE UTILIZATION CHECK SHEET

The check sheet for the Location Matrix File and space utilization routines is shown on Figure 6-5. The major elements are:

The development of the warehouse layout

The identification of all storage cells with dimensions

The loading of the matrix into the computer Location Matrix File

The receiving routine

The storage routine—storer or computer controlled

The rewarehousing routine—storer or computer controlled

The allocation of stock to orders from locations

The order picking path

The confirmation of withdrawal of material from inventory and locations

Cycle counts and physical inventories

The determination of travel paths for standards

FIGURE 6-5
Stock Location and Space Utilization Check Sheet

Warehouse location map

Identification of all cells

Sizing of cells
    Bulk pallets
    Pallet drive-through racks
    Pallet racks singulated
    Shelving
    Carrousel bins
    Bins
    Cantilever racks

Location Matrix File

Interaction of Location Matrix File with Inventory File

Updating the Location Matrix File
    Receiving
    Inspection
    Storage
    Rewarehousing
    Replenishment of forward picking lines
    Picking
    Packing
    Inspection
    Shipping accumulation
    Shipping

Warehouse location matrix screen layout

Cycle counts

Physical inventories

Standards—travel distances between locations
in the warehouse

7

Productivity Standards

Standards of productivity for warehousing operations should be incorporated into any warehousing operation of more than ten warehouse employees. In warehouses of this size, the potential increase in labor productivity will pay for the cost of the productivity, or work measurement, system.

Without standards of performance, warehouse management, both the manager and first line supervisors, do not know how they are performing and will generally add more personnel than necessary, especially to meet peak shipping periods, so that they can guarantee meeting the service levels of customers.

Past performance is generally a poor guide to the real productivity of a warehouse operation. It is well recognized that warehouse employees do work harder during peak periods but generally slow down during slow work periods.

In this chapter we will outline the elements of the computer system that are involved with the control and measurement of productivity in a computerized warehouse system:

The work measurement system
Work elements of warehousing standards
Examples of standard development
The Standards File

Work standards for order scheduling
The Transaction File for collecting work accomplished
The computer algorithms for computing productivity
Productivity measurements and reports
The audit trail of transactions

WORK MEASUREMENT SYSTEM

In any productivity work measurement system there are four components that must be accomplished. These components are:

1. *Standards of performance.* No productivity system can work successfully without a standard of performance for the operation under consideration. These standards must be developed and be incorporated into the productivity or work measurement system.

2. *The measurement of the actual work accomplished.* This means that a system must be established to report on the actual work done, in physical units, for the operation under consideration. If the actual work accomplished is measured, then by applying the standards, the total time at standard can be developed.

3. *Determination of productivity.* The total time at standard can then be compared with the actual time that was involved in the particular operation and the productivity of the operation for that time period determined.

4. *A follow-up system.* There must be a follow-up system to indicate to the management and floor supervision of the warehouse operation what the productivity actually was during a particular period of time. Obviously, this must be done as quickly as possible after the time period that the productivity was measured. It is of no use for a productivity report to be put out at the end of a month, or two or three weeks after the period in question. For productivity to be controlled, reports must be made during the week that the productivity occurred. Otherwise, the total work measurement or productivity system is almost meaningless.

WORK ELEMENTS OF
WAREHOUSE STANDARDS

The following examples of setting standards for warehousing operations are meant to be illustrative of the manner in setting standards, not as rigorous standards that can be directly used for a real-life situation. There will be a question of how far to go in setting standards, using engineered time standards as we present here, or to go to time standards as set by industrial engineering practices with stop watches and formal standard setting procedures.

If the standards are to be used for incentive programs or for disciplining the work force, then very rigorous time standards should be established. If the standards are going to be used by first line supervisors, however, for the control of their operation and for scheduling of the work of the warehouse, then engineered time standards are suitable. (The error in engineered time standards is about plus or minus 5 percent, as compared with industrial engineering time standards.)

The major elements of work in a warehouse operation are:

Work. Picking up or setting down a pallet, picking an item for a customer order, packing the order, and so forth.

Travel. Moving, either loaded or empty, either on foot or on a forklift truck.

Search time. The time involved in searching for a location or an item in the warehouse.

Paperwork (or control). The time required to read or write information necessary for the operation.

In a typical nonmechanized, noncontrolled warehousing operation, the percentage of time involved in each of the above tasks might be:

	Percent of time
Work	5
Search	5
Paperwork or control	5
Travel	85
Total	100

113

It is necessary, therefore, to recognize the high amount of travel time that does occur in a warehousing operation and to minimize this time by proper stock arrangement, proper layout, and mechanized and automated materials handling equipment, as well as computer assists in the scheduling and planning of work.

EXAMPLES OF STANDARDS

Storing pallets. (Figure 7–1.) In this example, a warehouseman on a forklift truck is required to pick up a pallet at the receiving dock and move the pallet to a storage location. The work elements of picking up the pallet, traveling to the storage spot, dropping the pallet, making a notation as to the location of the pallet, and traveling back to the receiving dock have each been allocated a standard of performance.

The variable here is the travel distance. If a Location Matrix file is used (as outlined in Chapter 6), then the distance between any two points in the warehouse can be defined in the computer and the actual travel distance computed.

Travel speed is dependent on the equipment used, the quality of the floor of the warehouse, and the congestion in the warehouse. It should be noted that 100 feet per minute is close to 1 mile per hour. An hour has 60 minutes; 60 minutes times 100 feet per minute gives 6,000 feet, or slightly more than 1 mile (5,280 feet). The speed of travel in most warehouses will average between 1 and 5 miles per hour.

Picking up a pallet is directly related to the ability of the driver and the speed of the vertical lift of the forklift truck. The storing of a pallet or setting it in a pallet rack is dependent on the height of the opening. For bulk storage or drive-in pallet racks, the drop time has to be increased because of the maneuvering of the forklift truck in narrow quarters.

In our example in Figure 7–1, we used a quarter of a work minute to pick up or drop the pallet and a travel speed of 300 feet per minute. To this we added a quarter of a work minute each for search time and paperwork, a total time of three work minutes for putting a pallet away. If two pallets

FIGURE 7-1 Examples of Standards—Storing Pallets and Cartons

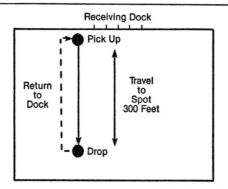

Receiving Dock

Pick Up

Return to Dock

Travel to Spot 300 Feet

Drop

	Work minutes/pallet
• Pick up pallet	0.25
• Travel 300 feet at 300 feet/minute	1.00
• Search	0.25
• Drop pallet	0.25
• Paperwork	0.25
• Return to receiving dock	1.00
Total	3.00

EXAMPLE OF STANDARD—STORING CARTONS

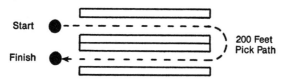

Start

Finish

200 Feet Pick Path

	Work minutes/trip
• Get cart	1.0
• Place 20 cartons on cart at 0.1 work minute/carton	2.0
• Travel 200 feet at 100 feet/minute	2.0
• Search for 20 locations at 0.1 work minute/location	2.0
• Place 20 cartons in location at 0.2 work minute/carton	4.0
• Note location of 20 cartons at 0.1 work minute/carton	2.0
Total	13.0 or 0.65 work minutes/carton

were moved at the same time, the time per pallet would be decreased.

Picking pallets. Picking pallets will have the same characteristics as for storing pallets. The work elements are: travel to the location, pick up the pallet, move to the shipping accumulation area, drop the pallet, and complete the required paperwork.

Replenishing a forward pick line with pallet load quantities. This standard, also, is similar in work content to the storing pallet standard.

Pallet-handling standards are, therefore, fairly simple to develop and, with a location-matrix system, very accurate in their usage.

Receiving. This standard is more difficult as the variables increase. The work elements, however, are:

> Get the paperwork from the driver.
> Check the bill of lading or packing list with the:
>> Items involved
>> The number of packages in the delivery.
> Move the packages or units off the trailer or from the dock.
> Confirm that the delivery is correct.
> Sign the driver's copy of the Manifest or Bill of Lading.
> Make out the receiving report.

Inspection and quality control of inbound material. Here, the work elements are:

> Open the package.
> Inspect the material. This is a very complex variable and is dependent on the number of measurements or visual inspections necessary to be assured that the quality of the material is correct.
> Count the number of pieces.
> Do paperwork for establishing that the receipt is correct.

It is generally inadvisable to have quality control personnel on a tight standard; their function is to ensure high quality of product, and not necessarily high productivity rates. The way to increase productivity in inspection functions is to take random sample checks, rather than 100 percent checks, and to ensure that production or procurement sources are providing the proper quality and quantity of material.

Storage of cartons. (Figure 7-1.) Here, the task is to obtain inspected cartons at the outbound end of the accumulation area of inspection, place the cartons on a cart, and travel through the warehouse storage area finding the locations for each of the cartons. At the location, the storer will place the carton in the location and note on a move ticket the location where the carton was placed. After all the cartons are stored, the storer will return to the inspection area. The determination of the travel path is a variable in this example but can be determined either on an "average" basis if there is a forward picking line or by using the warehouse location matrix to determine the actual travel distance. The rate of travel is also a variable. Carton handling is also a variable in that a small compact carton is easier to put away than a heavy large carton. We shall see that this can be taken care of for each SKU package size.

In the example, the standard time would be 0.65 work minutes per carton stored.

Order picking. (Figure 7-2.) Two examples for order picking are given. One is for picking orders from storage locations that are located in the bottom position of pallet racks. The picker will take a cart or pallet jack and travel through the warehouse picking the order in a scheduled sequence. As can be seen the major element will be the travel time.

The other option shown is a conveyorized forward picking line that consolidates the stockkeeping units in a case flow rack, reducing the travel time considerably. Search time is also reduced because of the increased density of the picking line. In this type of system, however, cartons must be replenished into the case picking line, which must be considered in the decision to have this sytem.

Generally, it is advisable to establish a forward picking line for cases, another for inner packs, and still another for pieces, as the labor saved by the pickers will more than pay

FIGURE 7-2 Examples of Standards—Order Picking

	PALLET RACK		CASE FLOW RACK	
	400 SKU × 4 feet/SKU = 1600 feet		400 SKU in 5-high case flow rack = 80 flow racks × 1 foot/flow rack	
	Pick path is 800 feet		= 80 feet ÷ 2 on both sides	
			Pick path is 40 feet	
		Work Minutes		Work Minutes
Get pallet		1.0		—
Walk pick path at 100 feet/minute		8.0	Walk pick path and return	0.8
Search for 10 line items at 0.1 work minute/line item		1.0	at 0.05 work minutes/line item	0.5
Pick 20 cartons at 0.2 work minutes/ carton		4.0		4.0
Paperwork at 0.1 work minutes/line item × 10 line items		1.0		1.0
Total time		15.0		6.3
Replenish cartons		—	20 cartons @ 0.1 work minutes/ carton	2.0
Total work content		15.0	Total work content	8.3
At 100 orders/day		1,500.0		830.0
At 200 orders/day		3,000.0		1,660.0
At 400 orders/day		6,000.0		3,320.0
At 800 orders/day		12,000.0		6,640.0

for the replenishment task. In addition, the concentration of labor in a forward picking line will lead to a better pace and closer supervision as the pickers are not wandering throughout the warehouse. The standard for replenishing cases is also shown on Figure 7-2 and in this example indicates that there is less labor involved in the flow rack system, even with the additional replenishment time.

The development of standards for picking inner packs

and pieces will follow the same procedure as the examples for carton picking.

Inspection.   All picked orders should be inspected for accuracy, either on a random basis or with 100 percent inspection. Standards for inspection can be developed and are dependent on the work station layout for movement of the inspector, the number of SKUs on the order to be inspected, and quantity of pieces per SKU to be inspected. Rigorous standards for inspection should not be applied as this is a quality control function and time pressure sometimes works adversely to the care that is necessary to ensure proper quality of customer shipments.

Shipping.   As is receiving, this is a difficult standard to develop, as the work consists of activities with truckers, ensuring that the right material is given to the right trucker, counting and checking cases of material, and carefully checking transportation documents. In most warehouses, this is not a high labor content operation and frequently can be ignored.

Loading cartons or pallets.   If the warehouse must load the outbound vehicle, standards should be established for this function. The work elements for loading cartons are:

> Get a full pallet and move it into the trailer.
> Take a carton(s) and place it in the trailer.
> Continue to pile cartons.
> Remove the empty pallet.
> Get another full pallet, and so forth.

For pallet loading, the elements are:

> Pick up the pallet.
> Move into the trailer.
> Drop the pallet.
> Move out of the trailer.
> Pick up another pallet, and so forth.

STANDARDS DEVELOPMENT

The development of work standards is based on observing the work elements that are necessary to accomplish the work function. The elements are generally obvious for any work function and include the work element itself, the travel elements, the control elements, and any other elements that occur.

The standards should be developed based upon what a normal person working at a normal sustained pace could accomplish during the workday. This should be done in conjunction with first line supervision to ensure that they are in agreement with the standard.

Idle, waiting, personal, and delay time should not be considered in the standards development. An "ideal" work standard should be developed so that the warehouse supervision will know their productivity based on the real work content of the job.

> *Idle time* should not be included, as this is a disciplinary function and is directly under the control of warehouse supervisors. The supervisors should be able to schedule the warehouse to maximize performance and eliminate any *waiting* or *delays*.
>
> *Personal time* such as breaks, wash-ups, etc., should be taken "off the top." If employees are getting paid for 8 hours, or 480 work minutes a day, 80 of these minutes might be allowed as personal time, leaving 400 minutes as the goal for productive work.
>
> *Fatigue.* Work elements with heavy labor content such as unloading or loading 100-pound bags of cement should be defined as fatigue-type standards. The time for the work element should be increased to give a fatigue allowance.

Each stockkeeping unit can have its own standard time for receiving; unloading; inspection; storing in cartons, inner packs, or pieces; picking; packing; and shipping. These standards can be maintained in the Product Master or Inventory File, or in a separate file in the computer. These standards should be updated as work methods or the characteristics of the SKU change.

FIGURE 7–3 The Standards File

		Illustrative Work Minutes
Receiving		
Truck driver time	Truck arrivals	2.0
Check Bills of Lading	Bills of Lading	2.0
Counting	Pallets	1.0
Counting	Cartons	0.1
Travel	Forklift truck	200 feet/min.
Travel	Walking	100 feet/min.
Unloading	Pallets	1.0
Unloading	Cartons	0.2
Inspection		
Per receipt	Receipt	1.0
Per SKU	SKU	Variable
Storage and rewarehousing		
Per pallet	Pallet	0.25
Travel	Forklift truck	200 feet/min.
Per carton	Carton	0.5
Travel	Cart	100 feet/min.
Packing		
Per carton	Carton	0.5
Per inner-pack	Inner-pack	0.1
Shipping—as for receiving		

THE STANDARDS FILE

Work standards consist of those elements that are consistent throughout the warehouse operation and can be considered as constants for the operation. These could include:

Forklift truck travel speeds

Person travel speed

Search time

Paperwork time

and are shown on Figure 7–3.

Variable work elements that are dependent on the characteristics of the SKU are:

Inspection of the SKU
Storing the SKU
Picking the SKU
Packing the SKU

and should therefore be integrated with the Inventory File or the Product Master File, by SKU.

ASSIGNMENT OF STANDARD TIMES TO ORDERS

Standards for picking orders can be assigned to each order during the Order Entry Routine using standard times for non-variable work elements in the routine and variable elements from the SKU data in the Product Master or Inventory File. As shown in the examples on picking orders for cartons from a conveyorized forward picking line, the work elements and times are:

	Work Minutes Per:		
	Order	*Line Item*	*Picking Unit*
Travel pick line	0.8	–	–
Search for line item	–	0.05	–
Pick unit	–	–	0.2
Paperwork	–	0.10	–
Total	0.8	0.15	0.2

We see that for every order the standard would be 0.8 work minutes for travel. For *every* line item on the order that is to be picked, the standard time would be 0.15 work minutes per line item for search and paperwork. Finally, for every *unit*— case, inner pack, or piece—the standard would be the time to pick that particular SKU, a variable that could be found in the Product Master or Inventory File. (In this example, 0.2 work minutes per carton.)

This routine is shown on Figure 7–4.

FIGURE 7–4 Order Picking Standards Routine

	Illustrative Work Minutes
For each order:	
Travel Pick line	0.80
Total	0.80
For each line item:	
Search	0.05
Paperwork	0.10
Total	0.15
For each SKU:	
Picking time	0.20

1. Determine picking time for SKU and package from Inventory File or Product Master File.
2. Multiply picking time standard by quantity on this order.
3. Continue for each line item.
4. Summate total line items on order.
5. Multiply total line items by standard per line item.
6. Add standard time for each order to picking time and line item time.
7. Print on order.

The output of this Order Picking Standards Routine would be the standard time for picking the order.

THE TRANSACTION FILE

The Transaction File in a computerized warehouse system contains all of the transactions by date that occur as well as the name of the individual who accomplished the work.

Receipts. The SKU, the package, the quantity received

Inspection. The SKU, the package, the quantity inspected

Storage. The SKU, the package, the quantity stored, and the location

Rewarehousing. The SKU, the package, the quantity moved, "from" and "to" locations

Replenishment of forward pick lines.	The SKU, the package, the quantity moved, "from" and "to" locations
Picking.	The order, the number of line items, the SKUs, the quantity, and the package
Inspection.	The order, the number of line items, the SKUs, the quantity, and the package
Packing.	The order, the number of line items, the SKUs, the quantity, and the package
Shipping.	The order, the number of line items, and the manifest or B/L number

The reporting of the transaction can be accomplished by entering the data into the computer from a piece of paper by direct entry from the individual responsible for the transaction, or by data-scanning readers that communicate directly with the computer. This is further discussed in Chapter 10, Equipment Interfaces.

The Transaction File is shown in Figure 7–5. Each of the

FIGURE 7–5 Transaction File Interactivity and Transaction File

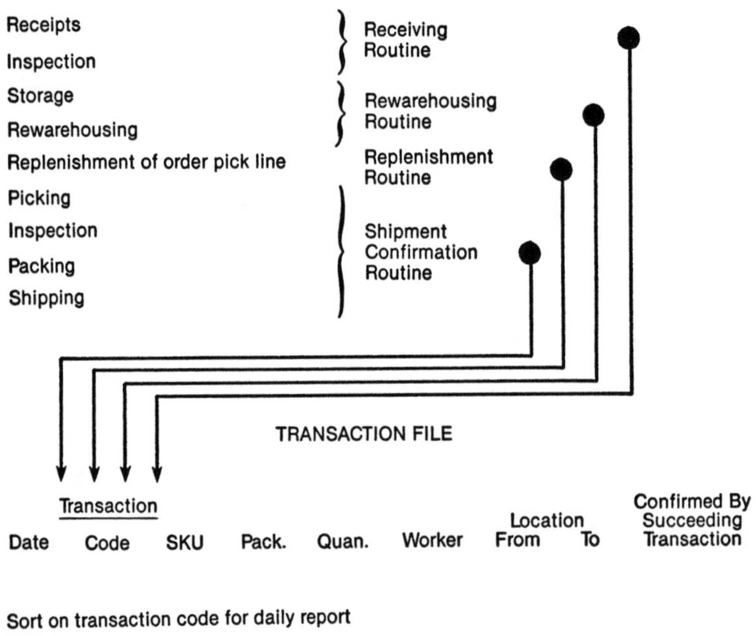

Sort on transaction code for daily report

transactions must be coded as they occur and the necessary identification of the SKU, the package, and the quantity handled must be entered. In addition, the identification of the employee who accomplished the work should be included to provide an audit trail for the work performed in the warehouse.

The Transaction File for a warehouse will be a large file, as every movement of the material will be included in it. This file could be printed out every day for the warehouse to indicate where errors have been made in transposing data, for example. It can also have a self-correcting routine in that it will not release an SKU from inspection until it has the same SKU and quantity put into storage.

The Transaction File has the other major purpose of having all of the work completed described in the file. It can then be run with the Standards File to provide a productivity report for the operation.

APPLYING STANDARDS
TO THE TRANSACTION FILE

The Transaction File will contain all of the transactions for material movement that have been accomplished during the shift, day, or longer period of time. These transactions are coded based on the activity that they entailed.

The Standards File has the standard data for each of the work functions in the warehouse.

The simplified algorithm for each of the warehouse transactions is:

Unloading. The quantities of the SKU package times the standard work minutes for unloading

Receiving. The inbound receipt times the standard time to receive plus the number of containers times the standard time per container

Inspection. The number of SKU packages times the standard time for inspection of an SKU package

Storage. The quantities of SKU packages times the standard time for placing the package into storage plus the travel time for each storage movement

Replenishment. As for Storage or Rewarehousing. Plus the time involved in placing containers or packages in a forward picking line

Pallet picking. As for Storage

Case picking. From the order; standard time per order plus standard time per line plus standard time per case

Rewarehousing. The quantity of SKU moved times the standard time for pick up and drop plus the travel distance from the original location to the new location

Inner pack picking. From the order

Piece picking. From the order

Packing. From the order. The package is based on the quantity of each SKU that is to be packed plus an allowance for adding dunnage

Inspection. Based on the number of SKUs, the number of packages

Shipping. As for receiving

Loading. As for unloading, except reverse

We see that after the standards have been applied to the transaction, the Transaction File will contain the standard work minutes that have been assigned for each transaction.

PRODUCTIVITY REPORTING

The next step will be to prepare the productivity report by sorting the Transaction File by transaction code. These codes could be:

- U Unloading
- R Receiving
- I Inspection and quality control of inbound material
- S Storing
- W Rewarehousing

H   Replenishment
P   Picking
K   Packing
Q   Inspection of outbound orders
T   Shipping
L   Loading
M   Miscellaneous activities

These transactions could then be accumulated for each transaction code, sorting by individual worker to give a report (Figure 7–6) showing activity by transaction code for each worker.

Another sort could be accomplished by worker identification number to provide a productivity report for each individual.

A third sort could be accomplished by product class to show the work accomplished at standard for each product. This could be useful for product cost accounting purposes. Finally, the Transaction File could be sorted by customer or user to show productivity at standard that could be very important for public, maintenance, or office material warehouses that must assign costs to each of the customers. This also has application for any warehouse that must charge back its activities to the end users of the product being processed through the warehouse.

We see that we now have reports of the work accomplished during the shift or day, or other time period, *at standard*. This must now be translated into productivity terms.

The actual workhours used in the warehouse must be collected. In most warehouses, this can be simply accom-

FIGURE 7–6 Productivity at Standard

Date XX/XX/XX

Worker No.	Trans. Code	SKU	Pack.	Quan.	Location From	To	Standard Minutes	Actual Minutes	Productivity
XXX	X	XXXXXX	XXXX	XXXXX	XXXXX	XXXXX	XXXXX	XXXXX	XXXXX
	X	XXXXXX	XXXX	XXXXX	XXXXX	XXXXX	XXXXX	XXXXX	XXXXX

plished by the supervisor's work assignment logs. The data from the standards reporting routine can be integrated with the actual work minutes used for each function, or for each worker, and the productivity of the operation calculated manually by the warehouse office.

A computer prepared productivity report could also be prepared by having the supervisor's logs, or warehouse personnel's time cards, showing actual time used fed into the computer for this calculation.

The results on the productivity calculations should be plotted, by day or shift, on a productivity control chart shown on Figure 7–7. This is absolutely necessary to supply the proper productivity information to first-line supervisors, where it will do the most good.

FIGURE 7–7 Productivity Control Chart

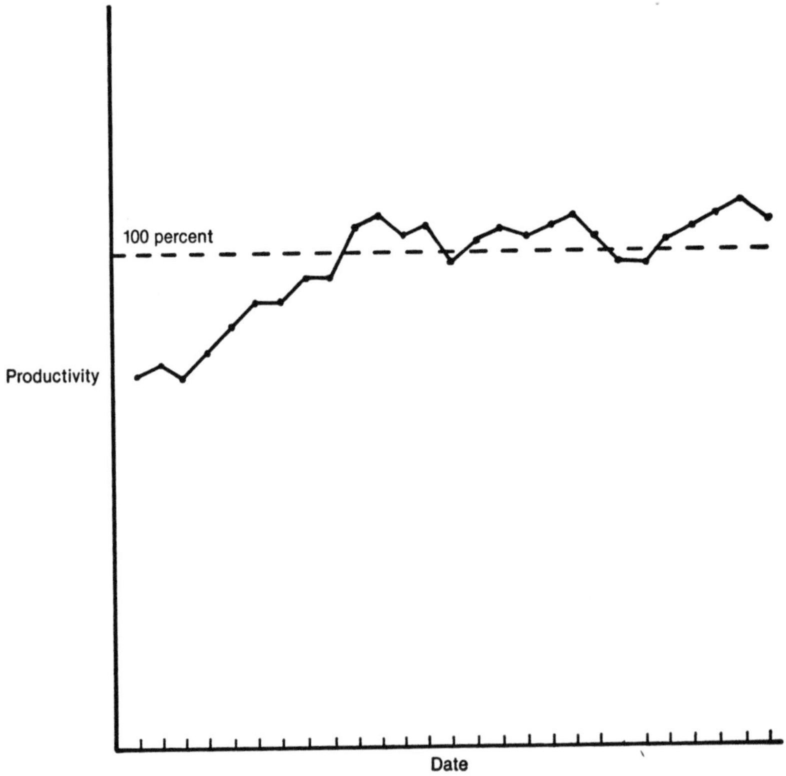

PRODUCTIVITY STANDARDS
CHECK SHEET

Figure 7-8 is the check sheet for developing a productivity standard and reporting system for the computerized warehouse operations. The development of standards for each of the warehouse functions, where appropriate, is the key function.

The next step is to design the transaction reporting system that will update the other files in the computerized warehouse system and interactively transfer this information to the Transaction File.

The Transaction File will show an audit trail for all material movements through the warehouse.

The Transaction File will run with the Standards File and Productivity Routine to supply productivity reports for each function of the warehouse.

The order-processing routine will include the setting of standards for each order going through the warehouse. These standards can then be used to schedule orders through the warehouse, assign the proper work force to the picking and packing functions, and to report on the performance of the pickers and packers.

FIGURE 7-8
Productivity Standards Check Sheet

Establishment of standards
  Receiving
  Inspection
  Storing
  Rewarehousing
  Replenishment of forward pick lines
  Orders
    Per order
    Per line item
    Per SKU
  Packing
    Per order
    Per SKU
    Per package

FIGURE 7–8 (continued)

Inspection
Shipping

Travel time
Work time
Control of paperwork time
Search time

Develop the Standards File
   SKU in Inventory, Product Master,
      or Standards File
   Travel time

Develop the Transaction File
   Coding
   Interactive collection of transactions
      in the Transaction File
   Receiving
   Inspection
   Storing
   Replenishment
   Rewarehousing
   Picking
   Inspection
   Shipping

Transaction and Standard File routine

Transaction control

Productivity reporting
   At standard
   For the warehouse—actual hours
      included for productivity

8

Work Scheduling

The computer should be integrated with the warehouse's work load scheduling procedures to assist the operating managers of the warehouse to plan, schedule, and perform the work of the warehouse. The computer control system must be tailored to the actual operations in the warehouse to allow this integration. In this chapter we will discuss the work tasks involved in a typical warehouse and the systems that should be developed for the computer to assist the workers, the supervisors, and the managers in scheduling warehouse operations.

The major factors to be considered in using the computer for scheduling work in the warehouse are:

Picking and packing of orders to meet customers' delivery dates

The availability of outbound delivery vehicles

Seasonality and work peaks of the warehouse

Pooling and consolidation of orders

Receiving and unloading of material into the warehouse

Inspection of inbound material

Storage, cycle counts, and rewarehousing

Replenishment of forward pick lines

Shipping

Semiproduction operations

Other scheduled activities of the warehouse
Performance feed-back loop

SPECIALIZATION OF LABOR

The function of a warehouse is to receive and inspect material, store and locate the material, pick and assemble the material to customer orders, and then load and ship the material to the customer or end user. A natural functional breakdown of the work of a warehouse can then be stated as:

Receivers and shippers. To handle both inbound and outbound material for the warehouse. These people should be able to take variable workloads in their stride and be able to deal with truckers and other personnel not on the warehouse payroll.

Inspectors. Inspection of both inbound and outbound material is an important function in most warehouses. These personnel should be very meticulous in their work and recognize the importance of verifying the proper identification, quality, and quantity of either inbound receipts or outbound customer or user orders.

Storers and material handlers. These people are responsible for the proper storage and location of material. They are generally moving relatively large quantities of material either by pallet loads or carts and must be meticulous in the storage and identification of material.

Order pickers. Pickers must be able to pick accurately and rapidly. Their work is generally well defined and they should be able to do the same routine tasks continuously without losing their accuracy or pace. It takes a particular type of person to be a good picker in a warehouse operation.

Packers. Packers have the responsibility for packing the material in an outbound container that will protect the material until it reaches the user or customer. These people should be physically dexterous and have the ability to plan their work in a rapid and efficient manner.

Workers should be trained to be specialists in a particular function in the warehouse. A good picker should remain as a picker as that is what he or she can do best. A receiver/shipper should remain on the dock as that person knows how to expedite inbound receipts and outbound deliveries.

Specialization of labor allows the personnel in the warehouse to find their niche, to develop the talents that are necessary for the particular function, and to improve their talents. It also offers job satisfaction to have both the responsibility and authority over a well-defined function of the warehouse.

Specialization of labor, however, can go too far. In many warehouses, job classifications become too narrow and there are jurisdictional disputes in the warehouse on who can do what tasks. The ideal classification for warehouse personnel is a single classification—warehouse personnel—with various grades of seniority or competence within the classification.

Cross-training of labor. The warehouse personnel should be cross-trained in the various work functions of the warehouse. This allows the flexibility necessary to run a warehouse operation by substituting personnel in the event of absences, vacations, peak workloads, etc. An employee should be trained in each of the functions of the warehouse and earn his or her stripes in being able to operate a forklift truck, pick orders, receive and ship material, and so forth.

While this appears to be a contradiction in terms, specialization versus cross-training, it gives each of the personnel a specialized task but with the recognition of the total picture of the work activities involved and the need for cooperative work efforts to make the warehousing system function effectively.

Designated areas of work. Figure 8-1 shows a typical warehouse and indicates the location of employees by work function. The receivers/shippers are confined to the shipping

FIGURE 8-1 Labor Organization in a Warehouse

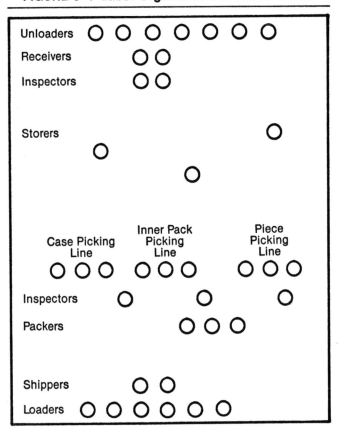

and receiving docks of the warehouse. Inspectors should be confined in the inspection areas. The storers, while mobile, are confined to the storage areas of the warehouse, the order pickers should be in a forward picking line area so as to have a paced work load, and the packers are generally in one area for ease in control of the work load.

This specialization of labor in a designated area allows easier and direct supervision, tight control over the work force, and easier scheduling of the throughput of the function.

In a large warehouse, a *labor pool* of workers should be established to be assigned to various tasks in the warehouse as the work load changes. This labor pool should always have a backlog of miscellaneous work to accomplish.

SEASONALITY OF WORK

A warehouse will have peaks and valleys in both the input to the warehouse—receiving and storing—and the outputs of the warehouse as expressed by customer orders. These peaks and valleys can occur in differing ways.

Seasonal or yearly basis. Warehouses that handle Christmas merchandise have a high seasonal peak of inbound material in August and September and a high output in October, November, and early December. An ice cream or beer warehouse will have high inbound and outbound in the summer months, while a heater or ski supply warehouse will have high inputs and outputs during the winter months.

The seasonal manning in the warehouse must reflect the work load of the warehouse. Generally, there should be a hard core of experienced and seasoned warehouse personnel on hand all year round. Temporary personnel should be hired to work under these experienced people to handle the peak loads.

The warehouse system must have simple operating methods and equipment to handle peak loads with inexperienced part-time personnel.

Weekly peaks. The end-of-month is often a peak time for many warehouses because of the pressure on sales to meet budget or sales commitments. These peaks, generally outbound, must be planned for and the judicious use of overtime considered.

As the monthly peak is generally in outbound shipments, the receivers and storers can often be assigned to the picking, packing, or shipping function during these peak periods, allowing a backlog to build up of material to be put away.

Daily peaks. Daily peaks often occur because of the methods or procedures involved in order taking by the marketing function. They are emphasized by having a rapid service policy of shipping orders within 24 hours of receipt. This causes high outputs for certain days of the week, and low outputs on others.

Here, the answer is cross assignment of labor to the picking function from the other functions, the judicious use of overtime, and the addition of permanent part-time employees during peak days.

These peaking effects often cause excess manning because of the propensity of managers to protect themselves from criticism by not having enough personnel to meet peak demands, thereby causing excessive labor during the lulls. Proper standards and work scheduling procedures should pinpoint these problems and the proper actions taken to (1) minimize labor costs while (2) meeting the service needs of the warehouse.

ORDER PICKING

The order picking and packing functions of the warehouse are generally the most labor intensive of all the warehouse operations. The order picking and packing system is also the one that is the most important function for the warehouse in its mission of supplying material to users and customers to meet their needs.

The major effort of the computerization of the warehouse should therefore attack the scheduling of orders through the order-picking and -packing function.

The computer-scheduling system must be integrated with the actual system for picking orders if it is to provide advantages in the scheduling of orders.

There are various picking systems to be considered in the warehousing operation. Some of these are:

Pallet in; pallet out. The warehouse receives pallets, locates them, and then, when needed by the customer or end user, finds the pallets and ships them out. The scheduling of the work is dependent on the computer assigning the proper location of the pallet and minimizing the distances involved in forklift-truck travel.

Pallet in; case out. Pallets are received but customers order in carton quantities. There are three methods for picking cases.

From storage racks on pallets. The picker will wend his way through the warehouse picking cartons from the designated pallet. This generally means long travel times for the picker in relation to the picking activity

Group picking. The orders are batched or grouped together and pallets are picked to meet the total quantity of the SKU for a group of orders. This minimizes the travel time of the pickers as the material is moved by forklift truck to a central area for sortation of the cases to the particular customer order. Additional labor is necessary, however, for the sorting of cases to a particular customer's order.

Forward picking line. Figure 8–2 shows a schematic of a forward

FIGURE 8–2 Forward Picking Line

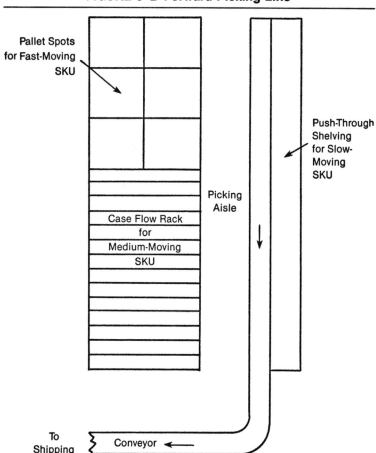

picking line. In this system, a small quantity of each SKU is assigned a forward picking spot and material is replenished to the spot on a scheduled or as-needed basis. The travel time of the pickers is minimized, but material must be double handled through the picking line, usually case flow rack. The savings in picker travel, however, generally offsets the replenishment time, especially if high-volume items are placed in the picking line in pallet-load quantities, thereby eliminating the need to physically handle these cases when replenishing the forward picking line.

Pallet or case in; inner-pack or piece out. Here, we have the following options for picking:

> *Inner-pack or piece-picking lines.* The stockkeeping units are set up in a forward picking line using flow rack or push-through shelving (Figure 8-2), which minimizes picker travel time but does require replenishment of the picking locations from inventory.
>
> *Shelving or bins.* All the material is stored on shelving or in bins and the picker must travel the picking line to assemble an order.
>
> *Group picking.* All demands for the same SKU are consolidated together, and the picker will pick all of the material for a group of orders, which must then be sorted to individual user or customer orders.
>
> *Zone picking.* Groups of items are kept in separate picking areas or zones to allow pickers to concentrate on a particular group of product. The output from each zone will have to be merged, or married together, for a complete order.

POPULARITY PICKING

Twenty percent of the SKU in a warehouse will account for 80 percent of the picks and activity of the warehouse (Chapter 4). Using this principle, many warehouses will have the most popular, or fast-moving, items closer to the output end of the warehouse. This minimizes travel time.

COMPUTER SCHEDULING
OF ORDER PICKING

The Open Order File contains all of the orders that should be picked in the warehouse. The Open Order File contains for each order:

The SKU

The unit or package to pick—pallet, case, inner-pack, or piece

The quantity to be picked

The location of the units to be picked

The standard time for picking the order

The shipping date

The Order Scheduling Routine then must take the orders and schedule them to the warehouse based on the defined operating procedures for the particular warehouse. These algorithms or routines can include:

Forklift-truck scheduling for pallet in/pallet out

Picking path development for order-by-order picking

Zone picking for picking from specified areas of the warehouse

Group picking for picking batches of orders

Short interval scheduling using standard times

Scheduling to meet carrier delivery times

FORKLIFT-TRUCK SCHEDULING
FOR PALLET PICKING

In high-volume pallet warehouses with a large number of forklift truck drivers, this system will closely schedule both inbound and outbound pallet loads so as to enable the forklift trucks to be loaded on both legs of the storage and retrieval function.

This scheduling and communications system will:

Maximize the utilization of the forklift trucks by minimizing deadhead travel.

Minimize search time by the forklift truck driver

Eliminate handwritten or keyed entries of numbers

Automatically maintain a performance record of each forklift-truck activity, if desired

Of course, the system can only be justified for:

High-volume pallet warehouses with over three or four forklift trucks working continuously

A warehouse with a balance between inbound and outbound movements

A warehouse with both inbound and outbound at the same end of the warehouse

As the computer system will be *directly* controlling the operation, redundant computer power should be available in the event of a computer failure. This system is shown on Figure 8-3.

The elements of computer-controlled forklift truck activity are:

A computer work file of pallets to be picked. The computer will sort the Open Order File for pallet picks and the scheduled time and location of the truck dock for delivery. This allows the computer to have a file of all the pallets to be picked showing:

The location of the pallet to be picked

The location to which the pallet should be taken

The time schedule for the pick

A computer file of pallets to be placed into storage. This file is built up from the receiving or inbound locations as pallets are received into the warehouse and shows:

The location of the pallet to be stored (from the location matrix routine—Chapter 6)

The location of the pallet in the receiving area

FIGURE 8–3 Forklift-Truck Control System

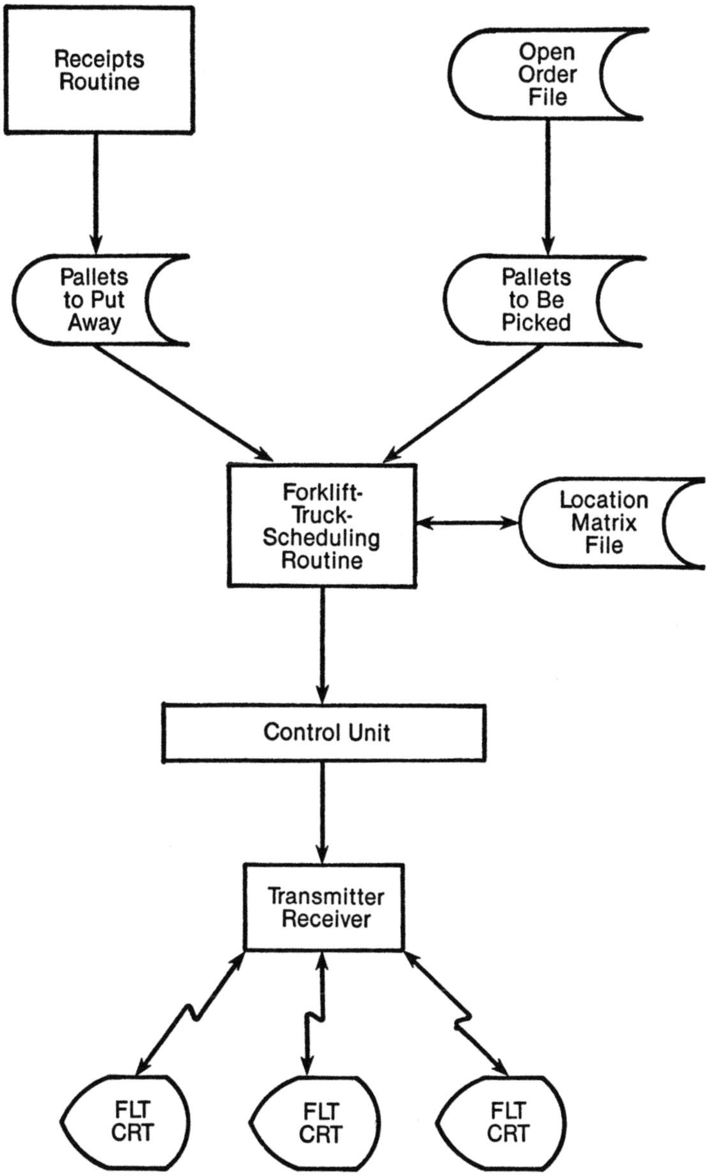

Using these two files and the warehouse Location Matrix File of all the locations in the warehouse, the computer will then assign storage or retrieval work to the forklift trucks.

The communications link between the mobile forklift truck and the stationary computer can be by:

> *Transfer of move tickets to the FLT driver.* The computer would make a list of the receipts and the picks and provide this hard copy of movement instructions to the forklift truck driver. The FLT would then move through the warehouse, picking the pallet, moving it to the shipping location, going to the receiving location, taking the pallet to storage, going to a storage location and picking the next pallet, and so forth.
>
> *Voice dispatch from a dispatcher with the computer.* The forklift trucks are dispatched much like taxicabs by a central dispatcher using radio. The dispatcher would send the FLT to the receiving area to pick up a pallet and deliver it to a location. When the FLT driver indicates that this has been done, the dispatcher would check the list of pallets to be picked, noting the location of the FLT and the time sequence necessary for delivery of the pallet to shipping, and dispatch the FLT to the proper location for a pick-up.
>
> *Computer-to-computer link.* The computer is linked with a controller that will convert the computer information to a radio frequency and transmit the computer instructions to a receiver on the FLT that would transfer the radio input to a CRT or LED display for the next activity of the FLT.

These systems work well *if* the warehouse is laid out so that material is received and shipped from the same set of docks in the facility. If receiving is at one end of the building and shipping is at the other end, there is little economic savings to be obtained by tight control over the forklift truck drivers— they will have to deadhead (travel empty) a high percentage of the time anyway.

In this situation, there is a possibility of using a driverless tractor-trailer train, a drag line, or automatic guided vehicles for the movement of inbound pallets to a storage zone, where the FLT is assigned for putaway. The FLT could also move ordered pallets to the tractor-trailer train or other equipment for movement to the shipping area.

PICKING PATH DEVELOPMENT
FOR ORDER PICKING

For warehouse order-picking systems in which the picker must pick items from storage areas, the computer can develop the proper picking path based on the location of the material in the warehouse as shown on each line item in the Open Order File.

Figure 8–4 shows the system for a computer to determine

FIGURE 8–4 Picking Path Determination

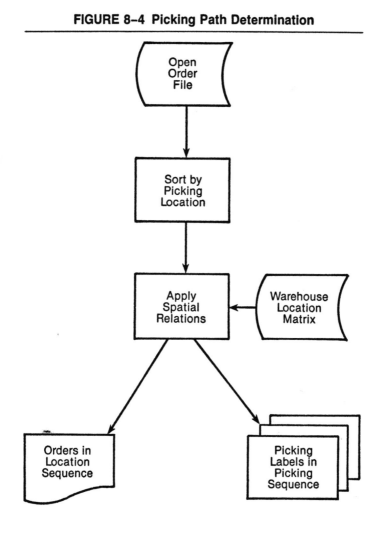

the proper picking path based on the location of material in the warehouse.

The computer will have the locations of each of the items required for the order from the Open Order File. These can be listed. The computer will know the spatial arrangement of the warehouse by aisle and cell from the Warehouse Location Matrix File (Chapter 6). The computer can then sort the required locations in the proper path for picking orders and:

Print out the order in location sequence

Provide picking tickets in the proper sequence

Communicate directly with a CRT or LED display on the picking vehicle indicating the path and the location and quantities to be picked

This system allows the picker to just follow the instructions on the order and not have to determine the picking path.

This algorithm is in common use for guiding narrow-aisle computer-controlled high-rider picking equipment.

ZONING OF ORDERS FROM VARIOUS PARTS OF THE WAREHOUSE

This is a similar algorithm to the picking path development, except that in this case the computer will divide the order into the designated zones of the warehouse and then determine the proper picking path for each zone, given the warehouse location matrix of the zone.

In this situation, the computer will also assign an accumulation area for final consolidation of the customer's orders. This can be a random location area in the consolidation area and should be shown on each zone's portion of the order.

The computer must also prepare the instructions for the consolidator. These instructions will show the order requirements for each zone so that the consolidator can check off the material from each zone prior to releasing the completed order for shipping.

GROUP PICKING
FOR BATCHES OF ORDERS

The computer can select those orders that will make up the batch that will be released to the warehouse. The Open Order File can be reviewed to determine those orders that should be picked based on:

> Scheduled shipping date
> Carrier availability
> Availability of personnel
> Etc.

From this the computer will sort by SKU and compute the total requirements for each SKU on a consolidated picking document. The computer will then search the Location Matrix File for the location of the SKUs that must be picked. The computer can then prepare a picking document or label, or transmit the required picking data to the group pickers on forklift trucks or with carts.

The picking document or message can be in picking location sequence to minimize the travel time of the picker.

There must be a location assigned to the batch for the group picker to deliver the material to. The individual orders will then be picked from the material for the group. This is done from a forward batch picking line.

COMPUTER SCHEDULING
BY STANDARD TIMES

If each order has the standard times associated with the picking methods on it, the computer can batch groups of orders to picking lines by accumulating these standard times.

The computer must determine the orders in the Open Order File that are scheduled to be picked, designate them as part of a batch, and then summarize the total of the standard minutes represented by the batch. This batch of orders for 100, 200, 400, and so forth, work minutes can then be transmitted to the picking operation for assignment to pickers. The picking supervisor can request a batch of orders for a given amount of time, say 800 minutes of work from the computer. The computer would sort the orders in priority while at the same time totalling the standard work minutes, cutting off when the required batch total of work minutes is reached.

This procedure allows the picking supervisor to determine the work load and assign people to meet it. It eliminates the slowing down of the work force when there is not enough work to go around, thereby keeping the pickers at a good pace.

SCHEDULING TO MEET CARRIER OR USER SCHEDULES

The determination of carrier availability will dictate which orders are to be shipped, especially in the pooling or consolidation of small orders to a geographical area. This is also necessary in dispatching user orders on a formal delivery time schedule. A cut-off time must be designated and any orders that have been received up to that time will be scheduled by the computer for order picking to meet the required delivery schedule.

SCHEDULING OF RECEIPTS

For a few warehouses, the input to the warehouse can be defined prior to the actual receipt. If this is so, the scheduled receipts can be entered into the computer in a Scheduled Receipts File. These expected receipts can be run against the Standards File for unloading and storage time and the standard work minutes determined for each receipt. This information can be provided to the receiving supervisor on a CRT or hard copy so that the unloading activities can be scheduled.

This system is particularly suitable for rail-car-supplied

warehouses, where a rail car can be received today but not unloaded until tomorrow. It also ties in well with company-operated truck fleets where the packing list can be transmitted to the receiving warehouse when the truck leaves the shipping warehouse.

The receiving supervisor, knowing the consist of delivery, can schedule labor based on the computer standards for unloading an inbound shipment.

SCHEDULING INSPECTION

The inspection function can be scheduled once the material has been received and is in the warehouse and in the accumulation area of inspection. The computer has had notification of the receipt and can develop the expected standard times for inspection for the SKU and quantities received, and then provide the expected standard work minutes total backlog for the inspection function.

The computer can also prioritize the receipts in terms of especially needed or required items. The Back Order File can play an important part here in giving preference to those items that are needed to fill past back orders. The next priority might be for those SKUs whose inventory levels are low and will be needed for the next batch of orders to be scheduled. The computer can then print out or display those inbound receipts that should be processed first in the inspection area, showing the location of the material if a random storage system is used.

Another simple method for ensuring that inspection meets the required lead time for the inspection of receipts is to color code the receipts on a daily basis; for example:

Monday—blue
Tuesday—red
Wednesday—yellow
Thursday—green
Friday—black

using colored decals. This gives a visual display of the aging of the backlog on noninspected material for action by the supervisors of the inspection function.

SCHEDULING OF STORERS

The standard work minutes required for storing material after it has been received can be computed from the Standards File if the put-away location is known. This can be used to schedule the storer's work load.

CYCLE COUNTS

Cycle counts should be continuously scheduled. Every day a number of SKUs should be checked for proper quantity in the proper storage location. Once the locations are determined, the total travel distance can be computed using the Warehouse Location Matrix File, and the standard time computed using an allowance for counting and checking each SKU and location.

REWAREHOUSING

The scheduling of rewarehousing tasks to maximize the utilization of cube is dependent on the need for additional space in the warehouse. During low inventory periods where space is not needed, rewarehousing activities are not required. But at high inventory times, the need to move material in and out quickly causes rewarehousing to take a higher priority. The computer algorithm for rewarehousing is shown in Chapter 6 and allows the computer, upon direction of the storer, to determine the cells whose contents should be moved from large cells to smaller cells to improve space utilization.

The computer, using the standards established for rewarehousing and the travel distances associated with the "move from" and the "move to" locations, can determine the total time necessary for rewarehousing. The supervisor can then determine the labor hours available and request a batch of rewarehousing move tickets.

SCHEDULING OF
PACKING OPERATIONS

Standards for packing can be determined for each SKU and for the quantity of material to be packed for an order. These packing work minutes can be determined as the order is received in the warehouse and can be totaled based on the release of orders to be picked. The ratio between picking and packing work minutes is generally fairly constant and can be used to determine the manning levels of pickers and packers.

For each batch of scheduled orders to picking, the amount of work minutes required for packing can be determined by the computer. This will allow the packing supervisor to schedule the proper number of packers.

DETERMINATION OF SHIPPING
CONTAINER SIZE FOR PACKING
OR FORWARD PICKING LINE

A function that can be placed on the computer if required is the determination of the proper shipping container for the packing operation. The cube of the SKU is taken from the Product Master File and as the order is entered is multiplied by the quantity of the SKUs to provide the total cube for the outbound shipment. This can be placed on the order so the packer does not have to make the decision on what size shipping container to use.

This system works very well in pick-pack systems. In a pick-pack system, the packers are eliminated and the picker is responsible for packing the items in the shipping container as the material is picked. The computerized determination of the size of the shipper eliminates the guesswork involved by the picker in determining the proper size of the shipping container.

REPLENISHMENT OF FORWARD
PICKING LINES

The computer can keep track of the inventory in the forward picking lines and provide the replenisher with the replenishment quantities per SKU as the picking line is depleted.

The picking location is an inventory location. As orders are released to the picking floor, the computer can reduce these inventories from "on hand" to "allocated to customer orders." If the reorder point is reached, this will trigger the computer to print out or display a replenishment order to the replenisher showing the SKU, the location, and the quantity needed. The replenishment quantity should be based on the size of the forward picking line and the size of the replenishment unit load.

SCHEDULING OF SHIPPING
AND LOADING

As orders are released to the warehouse for picking, the computer can automatically provide the work load requirements for shipping and loading. If material is to be loaded on the outbound vehicles, the standards can be applied to the quantities and the standard work minutes computed for each of the orders. This can then be transmitted to the shipping supervisor for proper assignment of loaders.

SCHEDULING OF
SEMIPRODUCTION OPERATIONS

Many warehouses have semiproduction functions that must be accomplished. These semiproduction functions include:

Returned materials. As material is returned from users or customers it must be received, inspected, counted, and returned to storage. The algorithms to be used here are the same as for any receipt of material.

Repacking material. Sometimes production or vendors make mistakes and the material is packed in the wrong container, or in the wrong quantities. Cartons must be opened, material removed and relabeled or repacked into different sized cartons. If this is a major function, standards can be developed and controlled by the computer system.

Weighing out quantities of material Frequently, material such as nuts and bolts are received in bulk quantities and must be picked in the quantities ordered by the customer. This can be accomplished when picking the order and should be reflected in the standard for picking the SKU.

In some warehouses, this is accomplished prior to picking by having a semiproduction function weigh out standard, often called for, quantities to be placed in the picking line. The computer can be useful here in determining the requirements for the new pack by reviewing past order quantities for the SKU.

This can also be accomplished for paper items, forms, and so forth, where the received quantity is not in the quantity that the customer desires.

Whether repacking by weight or cube, it is desirable to have the vendor or production source do this packing as it can frequently be done more economically than at the warehouse.

Cutting to order. This semiproduction function is essentially the same as the weighing problem indicated earlier. The answer is to precut wire, pipe, and the like, to standard order quantities, or to allow the time required for warehouse cutting for the customer order.

PERFORMANCE FEED-BACK LOOPS

The scheduling of work and the performance of work form a loop that can provide operating control information for the warehouse. For example, if the schedule calls for 800 standard work minutes of work for unloading rail cars, and the work is performed in 800 actual minutes and on schedule, then the performance loop is working well. If, however, the work actually takes 1,000 minutes, then something is wrong in the system; either the work standards are wrong or the workers are not working up to their capabilities. The productivity performance reports shown in Chapter 7 should be tailored to feed this information back to the operating personnel.

CHECK SHEET FOR WORK SCHEDULING

The check sheet of work scheduling is shown on Figure 8-5.

The first order of business is to establish the warehouse operating procedures for each of the functions of the warehouse. This means defining the work methods, the layout, and the equipment that is to be used for each of the operations.

Then, the computer system can be established for controlling these operations, considering the needs of the operating personnel, for computer prepared:

Paperwork
Schedules
Batches of work

FIGURE 8-5
Check Sheet for Work Scheduling

Establishment of the warehouse operating methods
  Specialization and assignment of labor
  Seasonality characteristics
  Methods of picking
    Order by order
    Pallet
    Pick then pack
    Pick/Pack
    Popularity
    Zones of warehouse
    Group picking
  Receiving
  Inspection
  Storage

FIGURE 8-5 (continued)

Cycle counts
Replenishment of forward picking lines
Shipping and unloading
Semiproduction operations

Computer scheduling algorithms
FLT control
Batch by time
Zone batches
Carrier or user delivery times
Size of container for pick-pack or packing operations
Replenishment of forward picking lines

Performance feed-back loops

9

Quality Control and Quality Assurance in the Warehouse

Murphy's Law: If anything can go wrong it will.
Note: Murphy was an optimist.

Quality control and assurance must be designed into a computerized warehouse system to ensure that:

Every item is identified and counted as it is moved through the warehouse operation.

Errors are corrected as soon after they are made as possible by having an audit trail of the movement from one operation to another with a feedback of errors made.

Every item is inspected for proper quality as it enters the warehouse prior to being put in storage.

Cycle counts or physical inventories are taken to ensure the accuracy of book inventories with the physical inventories.

Picked items are checked as to proper item and quantity prior to packing.

Outbound shipments are checked to ensure that the proper items and quantities are shipped to the proper customer or end user.

This means that the people, the physical layout, the handling and storage equipment, and the computer must be integrated into a total system that will maintain records of the movements of material and allow the correcting of errors as they occur and *prior* to their becoming major problems.

A warehouse is like a bank. The warehouse receives product that has a value and can be considered as a deposit. The dollars in a bank are transferred to the bank vault from the teller after counting for accuracy. In a warehouse, material must likewise be counted and checked before being transferred to the storage areas. As bank customers need cash, they write a check and a teller transfers the money out of the bank, after counting and checking, to the customer. In a warehouse, orders are received, filled by the order pickers, inspected for accuracy, and then shipped to the customer. The analogy of a warehouse with a bank should be kept in mind when developing the controls over a computerized warehouse system.

CHECKPOINTS FOR QUALITY
CONTROL AND ASSURANCE

Figure 9–1 shows the control points in a warehouse for quality control checks.

Unloading. When material is unloaded from a common carrier or an inbound vehicle, the unloader should check the container and, if there is obvious damage to the carton or package, should set it aside as a potential damaged item.

The unloaders of dead-piled or nonpalletized cartons often have to sort the cartons by their identification number. Care should be taken not to mix up cartons on a pallet or cart load.

Receiving. The receiver has a major responsibility in transferring "title" from the inbound carrier or delivery system to the warehouse. The receiver must be assured that the correct item and the right quantity have been received. Overs, shorts, and damaged items must be reported.

The receiving function is a major quality control check point. The controls on inbound receipts must be very tight,

FIGURE 9-1 Quality Control Checkpoints in a Warehouse

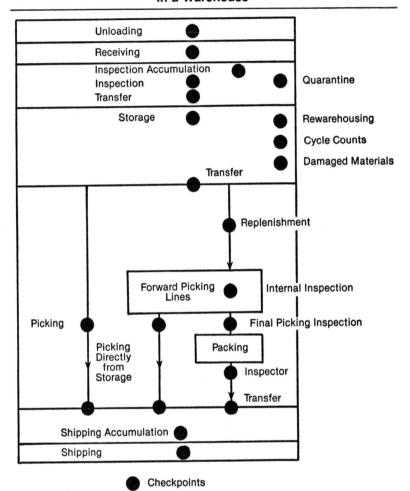

as poor count or poor quality here will cause major problems downstream.

Inspection. An inspection of the received material should be made to ensure that the item received has been identified properly, that the quality is up to the standard of the warehouse, and that the proper quantity of material has been received. The degree of the inspection can be:

Cursory for items that do not have much effect on the warehouse customers or users.

Accur.te count but cursory quality check. These are items from a production system that has had quality control inspections applied before coming into the warehouse.

Accurate count and defined random inspections for quality. These are for items that could have quality problems but generally are in the proper quality and quantity.

Very accurate count and 100 percent inspection. This must be done for expensive or items important to the warehouse or customers. This could include highly technical measurements or tests of the material.

The reasons for tight quality control on inbound material are:

Potential litigation from the customer or user if the material is not the correct quality. There have been major scandals involving companies providing poor-quality or malfunctioning items. In this litigatious society, the potential loss from a lawsuit from a consumer or consumer protection agency can far outweigh the cost of the quality control checks in a warehouse.

Potential costs by the end user. This could be a wrong item, misidentified, being used in the assembly of a product that causes losses of material or labor.

Potential pilferage. Pilferage controls must be included in a quality control and assurance program.

Some examples of materials that should have high-quality control procedures are:

Narcotics and controlled medications
Expensive high technology parts
Food products
Checks and important forms
Hazardous materials

The specifications for each item received by the warehouse must be developed and incorporated into the control system.

Quarantine areas. A physically separate and controlled area could be included for sensitive items that have not been checked by Quality Control, or for material awaiting the results of quality control inspection procedures that might take two or three days. This quarantine area can be located between the receiving area and the storage area to eliminate any possibility that noninspected material might be inadvertently picked for a customer's or user's order.

Nonchecked material can be stored *with* checked product in warehouses with good random storage location systems that have tight lot control and proper discipline. The computer is used to "lock out" withdrawals from the inventory until a quality control check is made.

Storage. The storer must identify the items put away, make a proper count of the material including the package quantity, and note the location where the material has been stored.

Any error in the reporting of an SKU number will cause an error in *two* inventory records—the SKU that was not reported correctly and the false SKU that was reported. Storers must be made aware of the problems that can be caused by misidentification of the material being put away.

Reporting the wrong location can cause mistakes by picking the wrong item or by losing material.

Cycle counts. Periodic checks of the inventory will help keep the computer inventory in balance with the actual inventory. These cycle counts should be scheduled frequently enough to allow close to 100 percent accuracy.

Rewarehousing. The movements of material from one location to another to improve overall space utilization in the warehouse must be reported accurately. The SKU identification, quantity and package, and the "move-from" and "move-to" locations must be accurate.

Damaged material. Damaged material should be removed from normal storage when it occurs. Damaged receipts should not be allowed past the receiving dock. The proper report form for damaged material should be developed and used by warehouse personnel to remove warehouse-caused damage to a new location in the warehouse to await disposition. Inventory controls over damaged items should be as rigorous as for good material. A new SKU should be defined for damaged material, or a code added to the original SKU to denote damage.

Replenishment of forward picking lines.   The transfer of material from a reserve storage area should be reported using the same principles as for any movement: checking the SKU number to be moved, the package, the quantity, the location moved "from," and the "moved-to" location.

Picking.   Pickers should be selected on the basis of accurate and rapid picking. Errors can be made by selecting the wrong item or by selecting the wrong quantity for the customer or user. Any errors made by the picker should be corrected by the picker, if possible.

Picking inspections.   Picking inspections can be:

Made by inspectors stationed along the picking line

The next picker in a forward picking line with zone picking

At the end of the picking line by a full-time inspector

By the packer prior to packing. This somewhat reduces the productivity of the packer, but could pay off in reducing errors.

Picking error log.   A picking error log should be kept for each picker. This log should show the number of orders picked correctly, the number of the line items picked correctly, the number of line items picked incorrectly because of wrong item, and the number of line items picked incorrectly because of wrong quantity.

The accuracy of each picker can then be quantified and reviewed with the picker on a scheduled basis.

The identification of the picker who picked the order should be carried in the control system, generally in the Completed Order File. This allows the determination of who made an error if there is a customer or user complaint.

Customer complaint log.   Any customer or user complaint should be kept in a warehouse log. The mission of a warehouse is to supply customers or users rapidly and accurately. Any complaint should be handled expeditiously and action should be taken to prevent a recurrence. The picker should be notified of the error that was made and be made aware of the cost of rectifying the error.

Packing.   Packing errors are generally minimal but poor packaging can cause damage to the items. Quality control centers on the ability of the packers to pack securely and rapidly. The proper equipment and dunnage must be available to the packer and random checks should be made of the work done. Complaints with regard to damaged material should be brought to the attention of the packer involved.

Accumulation prior to shipping.   This is a good control point for the final check of picking or packing errors. Random checks should be made by line supervisors and the warehouse manager. The actual order and shipping documents should be checked against the actual material being accumulated for shipment.

Shipping.   This final check should be accomplished by the shipper on transfer of the material to the outbound vehicle or delivery system.

Clerical errors.   Errors can be made at order entry in the SKU identification or the count required. A major source of errors is in the designation of the proper package. A customer might order 100 pieces, but the order can go through as 100 cartons of 10 pieces each. This could cause billing problems and additional costs.

COMPUTER CONTROLS
OVER QUALITY ASSURANCE

The computer can be a major factor in reducing and eliminating errors. The proper use of CRTs with user-friendly screen formats can force the double checking of entries by warehouse personnel or the clerical staff.

Receiving. A CRT on the dock allows the receiver to check the purchase order or production order and the item number and description of material ordered. This can help in assuring that what was ordered was received.

Inspection. The inspection CRT can also be tied in with the purchase order and production order system so that inspectors can have available the descriptions and specifications of the material, as well as the quantities ordered.

Also, the specifications for the stockkeeping unit can be programmed to show on the inspection CRT screen with the proper test procedure displayed. This eliminates the searching for drawings and specifications by the inspector.

The use of light pens, or touch CRTs, can force proper inspection procedures. The identification of the inspector should be included in the Transaction File to allow the disciplining of inspectors who make errors.

Storage areas. The use of CRTs, display devices, scanning equipment, and so forth, allow the storers access to the inventory and location files and can provide machine-readable inputs to the computer, thereby eliminating errors of transcription caused by writing numbers.

Picking. The use of machine-readable labels and CRT displays allow the proper interfaces with the computer to minimize written errors and to display information for the picking function.

Inspection of orders. Again, CRT displays of the original order can eliminate paperwork in the inspection of the order. Light pens can be used to "check off" correct items. The identification of the picker and the checker, and if appropriate, the packer, allow follow-up for the correction of errors.

Shipping. CRT displays will allow the shipper immediate access to the order and shipping documents.

AUDIT TRAILS
THROUGH THE WAREHOUSE

Many warehouses have audit trails for the transfer of material as it moves through the warehouse. This can be accomplished using manually prepared transfer documents and receipts. With the computer, however, these transactions can be recorded automatically through CRT or data input devices located in the warehouse and under the control of the operating personnel.

Figure 9-2 shows how this audit trail might appear in a computer-prepared Transaction File. The illustration starts with the unloaders who made an entry on a CRT or data transfer device that 2,000 cartons of Item 1234 were unloaded from railroad car No. 12345 at Dock A on February 1. The receiver, ABC, confirmed that the unloading had been accomplished and the material had been moved to Inspection Area B. Inspector LHN made an inspection and found 200 cartons were damaged or off-spec; these were placed in Inspection Area C; the remaining 1,800 cartons in Inspection Area B were released to put into storage.

The storer, DEF, on February 2 moved the damaged cartons from Inspection Area B to Shipping Area C for return to the vendor.

The storer also moved the good 1,800 cartons to bulk storage area B-14 on February 2.

Replenisher GHI took 100 cartons of the item out of B-14 and moved them to a forward picking line, Spot No. F-20 on February 2.

A pallet picker, NOP, also picked 600 cartons for Order Number 16872 out of location B-14 for shipment from Ship-

FIGURE 9-2 Quality Assurance Audit Trail

Operation	Date	Employee	Transaction	SKU No.	Pack	Quantity	Location From	Location To
Unloading	1 Feb.	RAN	UNL	1234	Carton	2,000	RR12345	Dock A
Receiving	1 Feb.	ABC	REC	1234	Carton	2,000	Dock A	Insp. B
Inspection	1 Feb.	LHN	INS	1234	Carton	1,800	Insp. B	Insp. B
Inspection	1 Feb.	LHN	INS	1234	Carton	200	Insp. B	Insp. C
Storer	2 Feb.	DEF	DAM	1234	Carton	200	Insp. B	Ship C
Storer	2 Feb.	DEF	STOR	1234	Carton	1,800	Insp. B	B–14
Replenisher	2 Feb.	GHI	REP	1234	Carton	100	B–14	F–20
Picker	2 Feb.	NOP	PICK 16872	1234	Carton	600	B–14	Ship D
Picker	2 Feb.	NOP	PICK 16880	1234	Carton	600	B–14	Ship F
Replenisher	3 Feb.	GHI	REP	1234	Carton	100	B–14	F–20
Storer	3 Feb.	DEF	REW	1234	Carton	400	B–14	C–22
Storer	4 Feb.	DEF	Cycle Count	1234	Carton	400	C–22	C–22
Shipper	4 Feb.	XYZ	Ship 16872	1234	Carton	600	Ship D	B/L8983
Shipper	4 Feb.	XYZ	Ship 16880	1234	Carton	600	Ship F	B/L46854

ping Dock Location D. He also picked another 600 cartons for Customer Order Number 16880 for shipment from Shipping Dock F.

On February 3 the replenisher, GHI, moved another 100 cartons to Forward Picking Line Spot No. 20.

The storer, needing the space in B–14 for another shipment, moved the 400 remaining cartons to a smaller spot in Aisle C, Spot 22, and reported this rewarehousing transaction.

A cycle count came up on February 4 and the storer DEF checked the inventory of Item 1234 and found that there were, in fact, 400 cartons in the location.

Shipper XYZ shipped Order No. 16872 for 600 cartons under Bill of Lading 8983 on February 4 and order 16880 under B/L No. 46854.

We see that we have a complete audit trail of all transactions that were accomplished on this particular item. This illustration might be more detailed than a "real-life" warehousing situation.

COMPUTER CHECKS
AND VERIFICATIONS

The computer system must be integrated with the personnel, equipment, and operating procedures of the warehouse. The computer system will have the missions of:

Ensure proper identity of the warehouse personnel. This can be by codes, passwords, or other identification of the employee.

Proper entry of information. Any keyed-in information can be checked by the computer as to its validity, and more important, the computer can be programmed to insist that the person who entered the number verify that the number is correct before the computer will proceed.

Checks for the accuracy of data keyed in. The computer will be interactive with purchase order files, inventory files, location files, and the like. Veracity checks can be made by the computer to ensure that the proper data is keyed in.

Trial balances and checks on inventory balances by accumulation areas. This can get a little difficult on a manual basis, but by using the power of the computer to indicate where errors might be made, can assist the warehouse personnel in maintaining proper records of movements through the warehouse.

Provide visual displays. These can highlight the important information needed by the operating personnel for materials in inventory locations, accumulation locations, on Purchase Orders, on Customer Orders, and so forth, so as to minimize errors and assist the warehouse personnel.

CHECK SHEET FOR QUALITY CONTROL AND ASSURANCE

Figure 9–3 shows the check sheet for the quality control functions for the warehouse. The major elements are:

1. Identify the quality control points in the warehouse.
2. Determine the proper interface for data communications with the operating personnel in the warehouse.
3. Develop screen layouts and user-friendly programs for the user.

FIGURE 9–3
Check Sheet for Quality Control and Assurance

Definition of quality control checkpoints
   Unloading
   Receiving
   Inspection
   Storage
   Cycle counts
   Rewarehousing
   Replenishment of forward pick lines
   Order picking

FIGURE 9–3 (continued)

Order packing
Inspection of orders
Shipping accumulation
Shipping

Quality control
  Screen layouts
  File formats

Audit trails
  Receiving
  Inspection
  Storage
  Cycle counts and physical inventories
  Order picking
  Inspection
  Packing
  Shipping

Selection of equipment
  Manual paperwork
  Machine-readable labels and equipment
    Bar codes
    Optical character recognition
  CRT entry

Data validity checks
  User responsibility
  Duplicate entry by user

10

Integrating the Computer with Warehouse Equipment

This chapter discusses the integration of the computer with advanced equipment in the warehouse for:

Moving material into, through, and out of the warehouse. This includes:

Conveyors
Forklift trucks
Tractor-trailer trains
Drag lines
Automatic guided vehicle systems

Storing material in the warehouse

Racks
Shelving
Automatic storage and retrieval systems

Picking customer or user orders

Pallet picking
Case, inner pack, and piece picking

Sorting and accumulation of material in a warehouse

Sortation systems
Conveyors
Palletizers and depalletizers

Controlling and recording activities in a warehouse

Optical printing and scanning systems
CRT devices
Weigh scales
Labeling systems
Metering systems

Advanced materials handling equipment is available for reducing the work content in a warehouse. Any warehouse operation can be completely automated; all that is needed is money. Therefore, the objective of a warehouse is to make the investments that will allow the best return on the invested capital in reducing labor costs.

The equipment in a warehouse must be integrated with the warehouse computer system. The computer is capable of scheduling, directing, and controlling the activities of a mechanical piece of equipment with the proper attachments, programs, and measurement devices.

THE IDEAL WAREHOUSE

Figure 10–1 illustrates an ideal, highly automated warehouse. Material is received in either unit loads (pallets) or in cases via a pallet or case conveyor. The cases are combined into unit loads, which could be pallets or tote boxes for movement to an Automated Storage and Retrieval System (AS/RS).

From this automated storage and retrieval system, the unit loads, either in conventional pallets or tote boxes, could be picked automatically to fill customer orders.

The automated storage equipment could also replenish case, inner pack, or piece picking equipment that could store the material. Customer requirements could then be automatically picked and transferred to a conveyor that takes away the picked material for a customer order.

Replenishment of the forward picking lines could be accomplished by depalletizers or deunitizers to singulate the cartons, inner packs, or pieces from their unit load. The material,

FIGURE 10-1 The Automated Warehouse

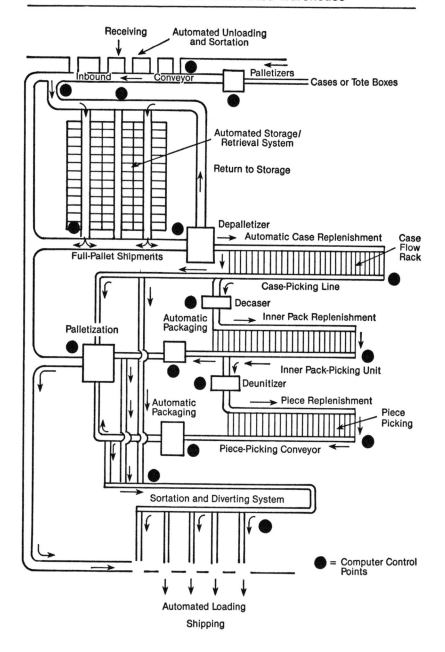

169

now singulated, would be conveyorized to the proper slot for the SKU.

The automatic storage equipment could replenish cases from either the pallet unit load AS/RS or the tote box AS/RS. The cartons would be depalletized from the pallets for movement into the case flow racks for singulated carton picking. This case-picking line could also replenish an inner pack-picking line using deunitizers to singulate the inner packs for loading into inner pack-picking lines for automated picking of inner packs.

In a like manner, the inner pack-picking line could replenish piece-picking flow racks using deunitizing equipment to remove the pieces from the inner packs, singulate them, and load a piece flow rack.

Picking would be accomplished by keying in the SKU and the needed quantity, the equipment would find the proper SKU slot, actuate an ejection mechanism, and the proper quantity of the unit would be ejected onto a take-away conveyor.

This conveyor would bring the material to automated packaging stations, where the units would be combined into shipping units. This would automatically be identified with shipping labels, in machine language, and would move by conveyor to diverting stations for accumulation to customers, users, or outbound transportation systems.

When ready for shipping, these conveyors would discharge into the outbound vehicle for delivery to the customer.

Most warehouses would not require all the elements of this automated system. Depending on the characteristics of the output, a system could handle:

Pallets only	Cartons and inner packs
Pallets and cartons	Cartons and inner packs and
Pallets and cartons and inner	pieces
packs	Inner packs only
Pallets and cartons and inner	Inner packs and pieces
packs and pieces	Pieces only
Cartons only	

A major problem in these types of systems is the nonstandardization of pallet, case, and inner-pack dimensions. An ideal system would have standard modules to be moved through the warehousing operation.

WAREHOUSE CONTROL POINTS

Control points for the "ideal" system have been indicated in circles on Figure 10-1 and include:

Receiving. Automatic unloading equipment could be used for transfer of the material from an inbound trailer or vehicle by use of conveyors or pallet handling, or case-handling equipment. A person would be necessary to set up the equipment, however, to handle various configurations of the inbound material. Automatic application of identification labels might be under the control of warehouse personnel.

Pallet storage diversion. This location would divert pallets into the automated storage and retrieval system, inspect the pallet for proper height, weight, and so forth, and move the pallet into the storage system.

Pallet withdrawal. This control location would receive customer orders for pallets or case replenishment needs for the case picking line, locate the pallet, and withdraw it from the AS/RS for conveyor movement to either the outbound locations or the depalletizing station for replenishment of the case-picking line.

Deunitizing equipment. The control system would identify the SKU, determine the dimensions and unit load (pallet) pattern, and instruct the depalletizing equipment to remove the required quantities of cartons and feed them to the replenishment conveyor. The pallet, if not empty, would then be returned to the AS/RS. Empty pallets would be returned to the receiving station.

Replenishment control system. The cartons would move along a conveyor to the proper SKU slot and be diverted into the slot for picking.

The carton picking control system would obtain carton-picking requirements for customer orders or for replenishment of the inner pack-picking line. These would actuate the ejection mechanism for ejecting the carton onto the take-away conveyor.

Inner-pack deunitizing. Cartons for the inner-pack line would be diverted to the deunitizer where the *inner-pack deunitizing control system* would singulate inner packs for movement to the proper inner pack spot. The *inner-pack diverting system* would physically move the inner packs into the proper cell. The *inner-pack ejection system* would then eject the inner packs to a take-away conveyor for customer orders or replenishment of the piece-picking line.

In a like manner, the piece-picking line would be fed by a deunitizing station with a diverting system for movement of the pieces to the piece-picking line.

Packing or unitizing stations would be required to control the placing of pieces into shipping cartons, inner packs into shipping cartons, and cartons into unit loads for transfer to customers.

A sortation and diverting system would identify the cartons by using machine-readable labels, divert the cartons automatically to the proper sorting conveyors and, after accumulating an outbound load, feed an *automated loading* system for outbound vehicles.

As can be seen, this idealized warehousing system combines automated storage and handling equipment with conveyors or automated transfer equipment with automated picking equipment all under the control of the computer or program control devices.

Let us look in a bit more detail at the various equipment in a warehouse and possibilities for the computer to control these pieces of equipment.

FORKLIFT TRUCKS

The forklift truck revolutionized warehousing operations after World War II. The forklift truck has the ability to horizontally move material rapidly in pallet loads to storage locations and then lift the material vertically for storage, thereby utilizing the height, or cube, in the warehouse. The forklift truck has now become the standard material-handling equipment used in any warehouse with high volumes.

Forklift trucks can be automated with computer control systems and guide paths to eliminate the driver. Automated Storage and Retrieval Systems are essentially driverless forklift trucks guided by computer controls for storage and retrieval of pallets or unit loads.

Forklift trucks operated by drivers can be controlled by the computer using radio dispatch equipment to tell the driver where to put away and retrieve material; this system is shown on Figure 10–2. In these systems, the computer maintains a storage and retrieval file of pallets to be put away and pallets to be picked. As the forklift truck completes a transaction, the computer will select the next transaction for the forklift truck based on the needs of shipping and the location of the FLT at the time, and then will notify the forklift truck of the next transaction to be accomplished.

For the smaller warehouse, LED displays might be used on the forklift truck with interfaces to the computer to provide instructions to the driver and to receive information on the transaction from the driver. Driven forklift trucks should generally not be used for travel distances of over 500 feet in high-volume warehouses. The cost of labor is high and can be paid for by the installation of draglines, tractor-trailer trains, or automatic guided vehicle systems.

DRAGLINES AND TRACTOR-TRAILER TRAINS

For high, constant-volume systems, draglines or tractor-trailer trains should be considered for movement of material. The

FIGURE 10–2 Forklift-Truck Control System

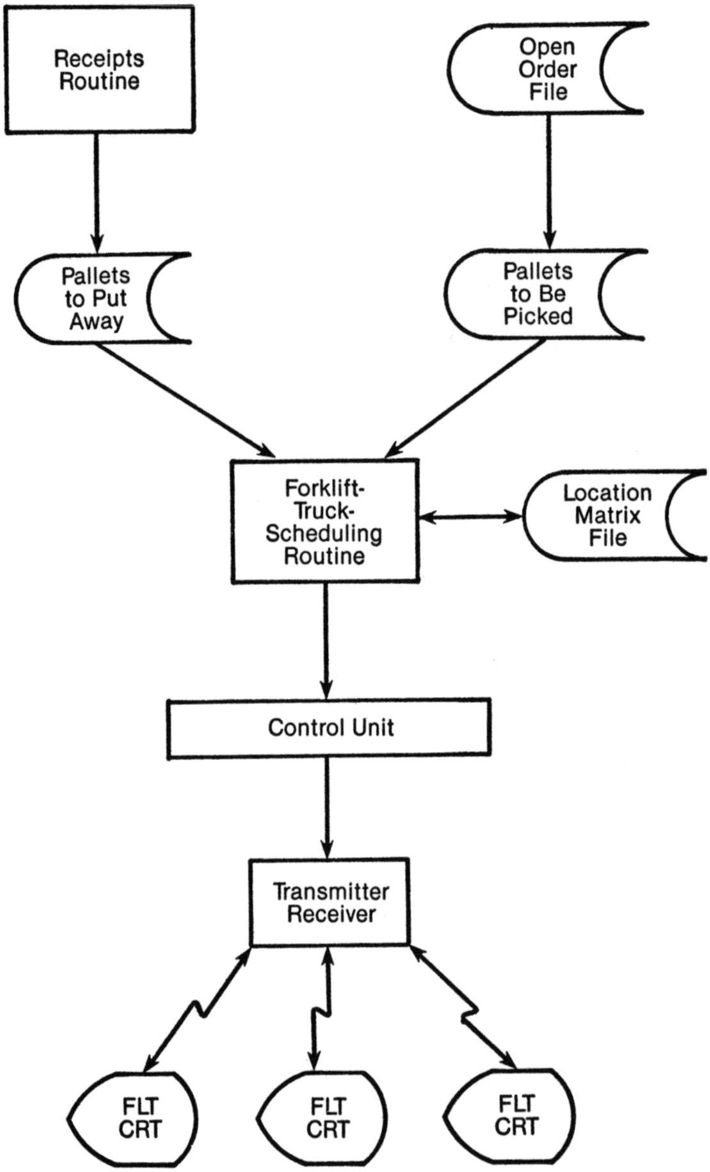

tractor-trailer train can be with a driver or computer controlled for movement to a station.

Figure 10–3 shows the schematic of a dragline or a trac-tor-trailer train, with the loading and unloading spurs for transfer of material within a warehouse. Automatic loading and unloading equipment can be used to eliminate the need for driven equipment.

Automatic guided vehicle systems can be installed for short movements or controlled singulated pallet movements in the warehouse. These pieces of equipment are self-powered,

FIGURE 10–3 Dragline, Driverless Tractor Trailer, and Automatic Guided Vehicle System

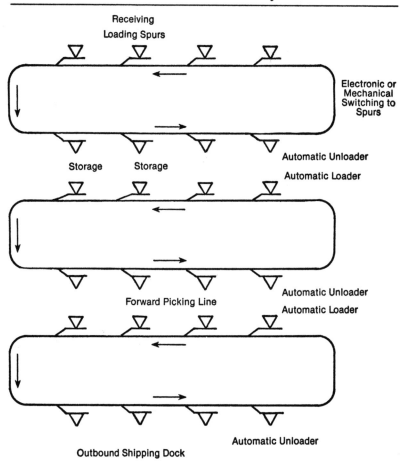

guided electronically, and programmable to move along various paths, stopping and starting as required by the system.

CONVEYORS

A high percent of the work content in a warehouse is in traveling, either loaded or unloaded. People move back and forth in the warehouse, on lift trucks or on foot, pushing carts or dragging pallets along. The reduction of travel time is a major objective in a cost-effective warehouse operation.

As noted above, draglines, driverless tractor-trailer trains, and automated guided vehicle systems are all equipment that can be used to reduce travel time in the warehouse.

Pallet and case conveyors can be used to reduce the travel time of people moving material about the warehouse. Pallet conveyors can be used for transfer of pallets from mechanized or automated equipment to the required location in the warehouse.

Conveyors can be used to transfer inbound material from trailers or production sources to the warehouse.

Conveyors can be used for transporting cases, inner packs, or pieces to minimize the travel time of the pickers.

FIGURE 10–4 Conveyor Sortation and Diverting System

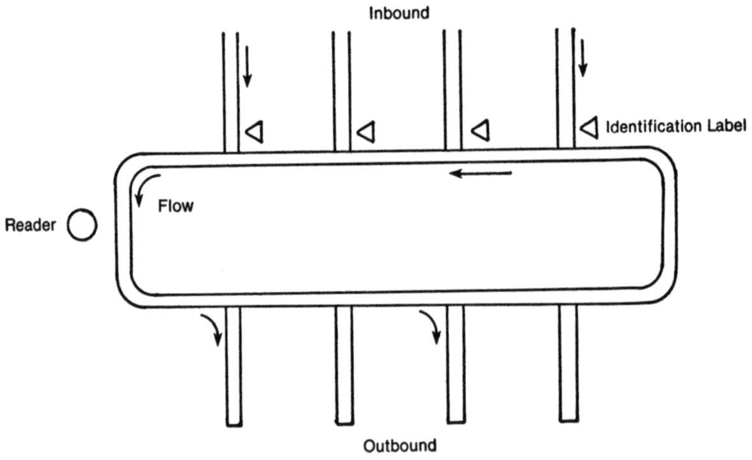

Conveyors can be used for sorting loads to accumulation areas by the use of diverting equipment controlled either by people or optical scanning equipment reading identification labels or markings on the load. Figure 10-4 shows a schematic of a conveyorized sortation and diverting system.

These systems can be manually or computer controlled. The cost of the equipment is such that the investment can be paid back in a short period of time.

UNITIZING AND DEUNITIZING SYSTEMS

Palletizers have been used effectively in the food, beverage, and chemical industries for many years. This equipment makes unit loads out of cases or bags to eliminate manhandling of individual small loads. Depalletizers perform the opposite function, singulating cartons or bags *from* a unit load. (Figure 10-5 shows the operation of palletizers and depalletizers.)

These pieces of equipment should be used in a warehouse operation to eliminate the manhandling of cartons or bags.

The computer controls necessary for the proper operation of a unitizer or deunitizer are:

The pallet pattern. How the items are arranged on the pallet base.

The tier pattern. How tiers of material on the pallet are arranged. Tier patterns could be different for each tier to allow the unitized units to tie together.

The dimensions and weight of the carton or unit.

With this information, the unitizer or deunitizer can unitize or singulate the cartons or bags.

FORWARD PICKING LINES

A warehouse must receive material, store material, and then pick material to meet customer or user needs. Many warehouses have excellent storage systems that maximize the use

FIGURE 10-5 Unitizers and Deunitizers

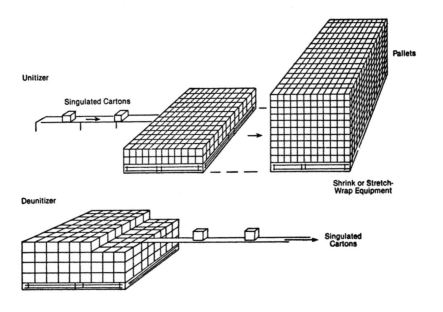

of the available cube in the warehouse, but force the pickers to pick the items from storage.

This is analogous to storing a case of gin in your basement and traveling down to the basement whenever you wanted to make a martini. The answer to this simple example is to bring the bottle upstairs to a *forward picking line* where we have all of the glasses, bottles, ice, and paraphernalia readily available.*

A forward picking line brings all of the SKUs together to provide a short picking face to allow minimum travel distance for picking customer orders.

*The author uses this example in his lectures on advanced warehousing and control systems.

Figure 10-6 shows examples of forward picking lines. A manual system is shown where cases are replenished to the rear of the flow rack and picked from the front of the flow rack. A conveyor system can be added to take away the picked cases.

Forward picking lines must be replenished by singulating the cartons, inner packs, or pieces and placing them in the rack position. This is the major difficulty in handling many

FIGURE 10-6 Forward Picking Lines

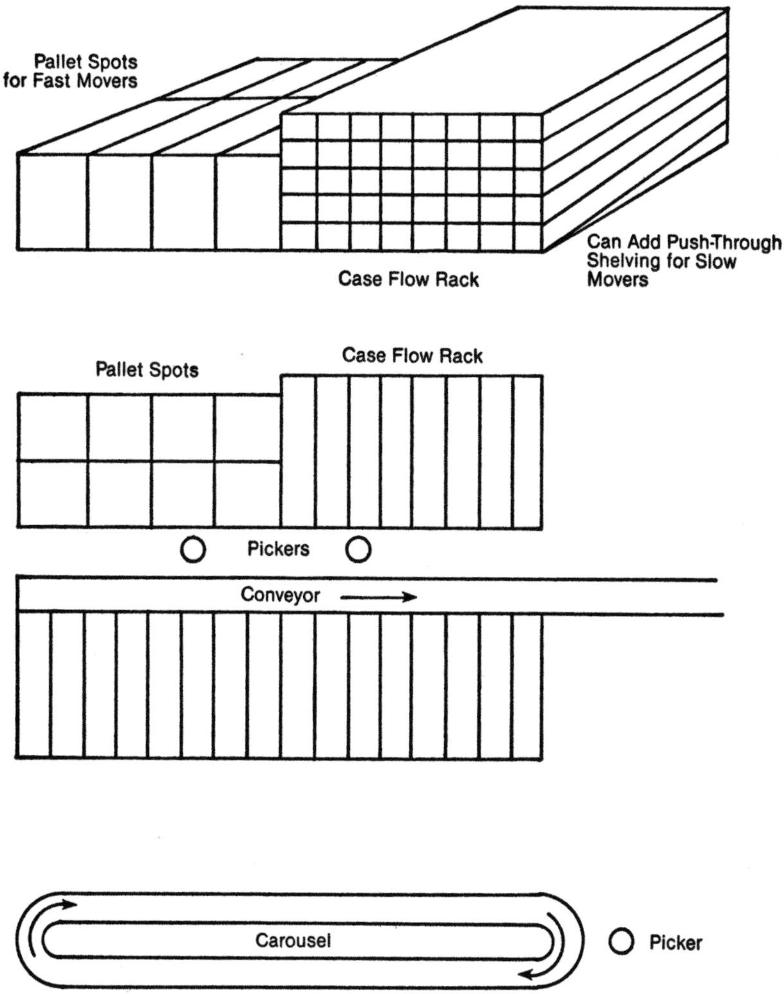

Pallet Spots for Fast Movers

Case Flow Rack

Can Add Push-Through Shelving for Slow Movers

Pallet Spots

Case Flow Rack

Pickers

Conveyor ⟶

Carousel

Picker

SKUs with varying configurations. However, with strides being made in deunitization, standard modular shipping packages, and advances in conveyor sortation systems, plus the increasing cost of labor, all indications are that very soon we will have more automated picking systems.

A major factor in the design and control of a forward picking line is to use the fact that 20 percent of the SKUs account for 80 percent of the total activity in a picking line. These high-volume items could be kept in unit loads so as to reduce the amount of replenishment labor.

The controls for the computer for a forward picking line include:

The status of inventory in the case-picking lanes

Indication to the replenishment function that the lane needs replenishment

The location of the SKUs in the lanes for the proper picking path

The control of automatic picking by providing the inputs as to SKU, lane number, and quantity required

The confirmation from the automatic picking system that, in fact, the machine did pick as instructed

OPTICAL SCANNING AND IDENTIFICATION EQUIPMENT

Optical scanning equipment has become common in the past ten years and allows the identification of a case or pallet or item using machine-readable codes for automatic identification, sorting, and diversion.

The item must be identified with a label or with the code printed on the container. The bar code or person-readable letter or number can be read and deciphered by an optical or laser scanning device. This is accomplished by the reader comparing the density and pattern of the lines with a preset pattern in the readers. For alphanumeric reading the reader will compare the intensity of the image with a prerecorded image of the numbers and letters of the alphabet.

Identification then allows the transfer of information from the process going on to the computer without the need for a person to write or key in this information.

The uses of optical scanning and identification systems are shown in Figure 10-7 and can be summarized as:

Receiving. Identifying product and the number of receiving units.

FIGURE 10-7 Optical Scanning and Identification

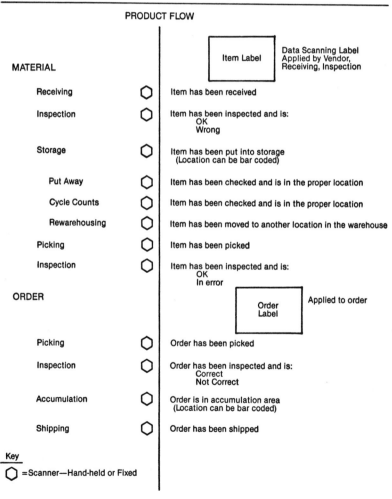

Inspection.   Identifying the product and counting the number of pieces inspected and moved to storage. (For inbound material that has no machine readable identification, the inspection function is probably the best location to place a warehouse identification label on the unit.)

Storage.   Locations can be designated with machine-readable identification codes. A storer can "magic wand" both the location and item as the material is put away, thereby directly providing the computer with this information.

Movements of material through the warehouse.   The scanning of the material and the programming of the scanned location allows the material to be identified, counted, and recorded without writing. Functions that could use this type of system are:

Cycle counting for the identification, location, and quantity of material in a location

Rewarehousing where material is moved from one storage location to another

Picking. The identification, location, and quantity of the material picked

Picking.   As an item is picked it can be scanned and the computer updated with the identification and quantity picked. Adding in the order number as a machine-readable code allows tracing and diverting of the order through the warehouse.

Inspection.   As the order is inspected, the inspector can scan the machine-readable order number to inform the computer that the order has been inspected. The identification of the inspector and time or date can also be automatically entered into the computer.

Accumulation areas.   In a like manner, the move of the order to the accumulation area can be scanned, informing the computer that the order is now in the accumulation area and, perhaps, with a specific location in the area.

Shipping. The identification of the order and the quantity of the packages or containers as they are loaded into an outbound vehicle provides another direct input into the computer for the shipping transaction.

THE PAPERLESS
WAREHOUSE

As can be seen, in integrating the optical-scanning function with the automated equipment that is available, the paperwork can virtually be eliminated from a warehouse operation.

As material is received it will be printed or labeled with machine-readable codes. As the material moves through the warehouse, these codes will be read and material can be located and retrieved using the codes for both the material and the storage locations.

When orders are received, the material can be located, picked automatically, and transferred, using conveyors or automatic mobile equipment, to the proper outbound station using diverting equipment actuated by the optical scanning system.

OTHER EQUIPMENT FOR THE ADVANCED
AND AUTOMATED WAREHOUSE

Automated labeling equipment. These pieces of equipment automatically prepare an SKU or shipping label and place it on a carton or container.

Automatic packaging equipment. These pieces of equipment automatically take small items and place them into a carton or container.

Automatic package-closing and sealing equipment. They can measure the size of the carton and apply the proper strap, glue, or staples to close the carton.

Automatic stretch or shrink-wrap equipment.   These pieces of equipment will wrap a pallet, container, or piece on a tray with stretch- or shrink-wrap film to provide a secure package or unit load.

Automatic weighing and labeling equipment.   These pieces of equipment automatically weigh a container, perhaps as it is moving on a conveyor, and record the weight either in the computer or on a self-adhesive label for application to the package or container.

Automatic weighing and computation of shipping charges.   This equipment can weigh, compute the transportation charges, and apply a label to the package or container for small-parcel shipments.

CHECK SHEET FOR INTEGRATING THE COMPUTER WITH ADVANCED WAREHOUSE EQUIPMENT

Figure 10–8 shows the check sheet for integrating the computer with advanced warehousing equipment.

FIGURE 10–8
Check Sheet for Integrating the Computer with Advanced Warehouse Equipment

Determination of material movements and volumes
    through the warehousing operation
    Receiving
    Inspection (inbound)
    Storage
    Picking
    Inspection (outbound)
    Packing
    Accumulation
    Shipping

Evaluation of mechanized and automated equipment
    Costs
    Savings

FIGURE 10–8 (continued)

Conveyors
  Pallet
  Case
  Piece
  Automated sorting

Automated mobile equipment
  Forklift truck control
  Drag lines
  Driverless tractor-trailer trains
  Automatic guided-vehicle systems

Automated storage and handling equipment
  Case flow racks
  Automated storage and retrieval systems
    Pallets
    Totes
    Pieces
  Automated picking systems
    Case flow rack
    Piece flow rack

Other automated equipment
  Case sealers
  Case labelers
  Parcel manifest systems
  Automatic weighing systems
  Carton-making equipment
  Palletizers and depalletizers

Data scanning equipment

Integration of computer with equipment
  Systems specifications
  Programming, testing, and debugging

11

Shipping Schedules and
Transportation Arrangements

Two major functions of the warehouse will be discussed in this chapter:

1. The transportation arrangements for getting the material to the customer or end user. This means the controls over common, contract, or private carriers.
2. The physical arrangements for shipping material out of the warehouse and the computer controls necessary for proper shipment accumulation and transfer of the shipment to the delivery vehicle.

The transportation arrangements often dictate the scheduling of order-picking in the warehouse. This is especially true for the pooling of small shipments so as to get better freight rates. It is also necessary for contract carrier arrangements and for private truck fleet operations.

OPEN ORDER FILE

The Open Order Screen Format as shown on Figure 11–1 displays the Open Order File that contains all of the orders available for shipment by the warehouse.

FIGURE 11-1 Screen Format for Open Order

```
                        OPEN ORDER FILE

 Our Order No. XXXXXX          Customer Order No. XXXXXXX
 Customer Ship to             Customer Bill to
 Name  XXXXXXXXXXXXXXXXXXX    Name  XXXXXXXXXXXXXXXXXXX
 Adr.  XXXXXXXXXXXXXXXXXX     Adr.  XXXXXXXXXXXXXXXXXX
 City  XXXXXXXXXXX State XX   City  XXXXXXXXXXX State XX
 Zip   XXXXX                  Zip   XXXXX
 Date Requested XX/XX/XX

                                                    Work
 Line Item No.  Description  Quan. Unit  Loc.  Wt.  Cube Min.

  1   XXXXXXX XXXXXXXXXX XXXX  XXXX XXXX  XXXX  XXXX XXXX
  2   XXXXXXX XXXXXXXXXX XXXX  XXXX XXXX  XXXX  XXXX XXXX
  3   XXXXXXX XXXXXXXXXX XXXX  XXXX XXXX  XXXX  XXXX XXXX
  4   XXXXXXX XXXXXXXXXX XXXX  XXXX XXXX  XXXX  XXXX XXXX
 Total Items: XXXXXXX                     XXXX  XXXX XXXX
```

Every order can be cubed out or weighed out. Every SKU in the warehouse should have its dimensions—length, width, and height—and weight per unit defined in the Product Master or Inventory File. This allows the computation of the cube and weight of each package of the SKU. The computer can then calculate the cube or weight of each order by multiplying the SKU units on the order by the cube per unit or the weight per unit, and adding in a tare factor, if necessary, for pallets or packing material.

The Open Order File should also show the scheduled ship date for each of the customer or user orders. This allows the prioritizing of outbound shipments and will often, when used in conjunction with weight or cube data, form the basis for scheduling delivery vehicles for outbound shipments.

SCHEDULING OF SHIPMENTS

This routine is necessary to determine the picking and shipping work loads of the warehouse and uses the Open Order File. The routine will take into consideration:

Scheduled ship date. For many warehouses, this is the only routine that is needed. Incoming orders are assigned a ship date, which is generally within a day or two of receipt. The orders with assigned ship dates are then sent to the warehouse for shipment.

This system is prevalent for small shippers using small parcel carriers where pooling or consolidation of shipments is not economically feasible because the volume does not warrant the necessary controls.

It is also the system that most small warehouses will use for supplying orders to end users who order material and require quick delivery.

Carrier availability.   This interface is necessary for pooling shipments, the scheduling of dispatched shipments, and the operation of a private truck fleet.

Emergency or "rush" shipments.   Bona fide emergency shipments must be expedited to the customer or end user. In the order entry process the decision has to be made on the validity of the emergency or rush situation. There is a common tendency for all orders to become rush or emergency. Once the emergency has been validated, however, the order must follow a path that gets the order picked, packed (if necessary), and scheduled for shipment to meet the customer's need.

A typical order-scheduling CRT screen is shown in Figure 11-2. In this illustration the Open Order File is run in date sequence and shows the total warehouse picking work load in standard work minutes. In this example the run indicates that the total picking work load is made up of approximately 3.7 percent for rush or emergency orders; 40.8 percent for today; 37 percent for next-day picking; and 18.5 percent for the following day. The capacity of the warehouse dictates that it can only fulfill the rush or emergency pickings plus all the orders scheduled for today. Therefore, this volume will be issued to the warehouse for the day's work. The run also indicates that there is no need for overtime as the balance of the picking workload can account for work for about 85 percent of the warehouse labor force for the next day. This, plus the new

FIGURE 11-2 Shipment Scheduling From Open Order File

Scheduled Ship Date	Ship Date	Order No.	Cust.	Loc.	Standard Work Min.	Percent
Today	R	XXXXXX	XXXX	XXX	XX.X	
	E	XXXXXX	XXXX	XXX	XX.X	
	R	XXXXXX	XXXX	XXX	XX.X	
	E	XXXXXX	XXXX	XXX	XX.X	
					200.0	3.7
Today	XX/XX/XX	XXXX	XXXX	XXX	XX.X	
	XX/XX/XX	XXXX	XXXX	XXX	XX.X	
	XX/XX/XX	XXXX	XXXX	XXX	XX.X	
					2,203.0	40.8
Tomorrow	XX/XX/XX	XXXX	XXXX	XXX	XX.X	
	XX/XX/XX	XXXX	XXXX	XXX	XX.X	
	XX/XX/XX	XXXX	XXXX	XXX	XX.X	
					2,000.0	37.0
Next Day	XX/XX/XX	XXXX	XXXX	XXX	XX.X	
	XX/XX/XX	XXXX	XXXX	XXX	XX.X	
					1,000.0	18.5
Total					5,403.0	100.0

orders that come in, should fill out the following day's work load.

POOLING

Pooling is necessary to consolidate small orders into one large shipment to take advantage of reduced transportation charges for one large shipment, rather than many small shipments.

In a pooling routine, the Open Order File must be sorted by the destination of the shipment by using the ZIP code or the state and city of the consignee. Other geographic codes could be established for a particular distribution area and indicated on the order when it is entered into the Open Order File.

Figure 11-3 shows the pigeonhole approach for the pooling of shipments in a manual system. Pigeonholes are designated for each destination that can be pooled. As orders are received, the orders are cubed or weighed out and placed in

FIGURE 11-3 Pooling Routine—Pigeonholes and CRT Screen

PIGEONHOLES FOR POOLING

Seattle	Portland	San Francisco	Los Angeles	Denver
Phoenix	Kansas City	St. Louis	Minneapolis	Chicago
Dallas	Atlanta	New York	Boston	Buffalo

CRT SCREEN FOR POOLING

Denver Pool

Total Weight XXXX Total Cube XXXX
Oldest Order XX/XX/XX

Order No.	Customer	Ship Date	Cube	Weight	Standard Work Min.
XXXX	XXXXX	XX/XX/XX	XXX	XXXX	XXXX
XXXX	XXXXX	XX/XX/XX	XXX	XXXX	XXXX
XXXX	XXXXX	XX/XX/XX	XXX	XXXX	XXXX
Total			XXX	XXXX	XXXX

the proper hole, noting the cumulative weight or cube of orders. When the cumulative total reaches the cube or weight of a full truckload, the carrier is called, a date is set for pickup, and the orders are released to the warehouse for picking.

In a like manner, the computer would accumulate the weight or cube of the orders for every destination code. When the cube or weight reaches a predetermined level, the computer will indicate this fact on a CRT for the transportation scheduler of the warehouse, who will then order the vehicle. (This screen is also shown on Figure 11-3.)

It should be noted that some products cube out before they weigh out in a transportation system. Bulky items, such as lawn furniture, do not weigh much but require a lot of cubic space. A full truck load of this type of material will therefore, cube out before the weight limit is reached. If one were shipping batteries or lead ingots, these items would reach the weight limit of a full truckload of 40,000 pounds long before they would cube out.

It should also be noted that most warehouses can only hold orders for a limited amount of time or customers will not be pleased with the service they are getting. The computer system must therefore check the ship date of the oldest order in the pooling batch. A designated number of days must be established for the holding of orders. When this date is reached, the total batch of orders must be picked and shipped and a new running total started.

CARRIER SCHEDULING

The scheduling of outbound carriers can be a major responsibility of a warehouse operation to ensure that shipments are made to meet the customer or user required delivery date. The major transportation modes that are available to most warehouses are:

Rail. Many warehouses are continuing to ship by rail for large-volume, long-distance movements. Rail-car scheduling has to consider the leadtime necessary for the railroad to schedule cars to meet the shipping schedule. This generally implies that a longer leadtime is required to obtain rail cars than for the other modes of shipment.

Common carrier—truck.   Most trucking companies require notification of pickups or needed trailers at least a half a day ahead of schedule. Many truckers do operate on a very tight schedule, but it is generally advisable to plan the workload of the warehouse and the needs for trucks and trailers at least a day ahead to ensure that trailers are available to meet the outbound demands of the warehouse.

Private trucking.   If a company operates its own private truck fleet, the scheduling of the fleet is another added factor to be considered in the warehouse operation. To operate properly, a private truck fleet must have a balance of outbound and inbound loads in the trucking system. This means that the truck fleet schedule might dictate when shipments are going to be made out of the warehouse. The outbound volumes must be developed by manipulation of the Open Order File given the availability of the private truck fleet.

In most situations, common carriers are used to supplement a private truck fleet to meet customer service requirements.

Contract carriers.   Many companies use contract carriers to move material from a warehouse to a particular geographical area. For contract carriage to be economic, there has to be sufficient volume moving from the warehouse location to the designated region and, again, the contract carrier must be scheduled sometimes two or more days in advance.

Air shipments.   Shipping by air is more costly but minimizes the time between the shipment and receipt of the material by the customer. Air shipping can also reduce the costs of regional warehouses, scattered inventories, and to some extent, packaging costs.

Small parcel shipment companies.   These carriers provide excellent service throughout the United States and have scheduled pickup service. The carrier will often leave trailers for the direct loading of the outbound shipments.

COMPUTER INTERFACE
WITH THE TRANSPORTATION
SCHEDULER

Figure 11-4 shows the CRT format for the transportation scheduling system. The screen shows:

Ship date
Order number
Weight (or cube)
Destination

This information is then reviewed by the transportation scheduler. As trailers are ordered, the scheduler will notify the computer that the transportation equipment has been ordered; the computer can then release the batch of orders to picking and packing.

Often a particular loading dock must be assigned for the assembly or accumulation of orders for the carrier involved. This schedule board for both inbound and outbound trucks is also shown on Figure 11-4.

This allows the picking document to show the outbound shipping dock for the picked material; this is especially important for movement of pallets from storage direct to the outbound accumulation area.

PHYSICAL FACILITIES
FOR SHIPPING

The shipping dock should have areas behind each dock for the accumulation of shipments for that dock. These areas should be located on the warehouse location matrix for development of actual travel distances from storage locations.

If possible, shipments should be loaded directly into the outbound trailer.

FIGURE 11-4 Truck Dock Schedule Board and CRT Screen for Shipping

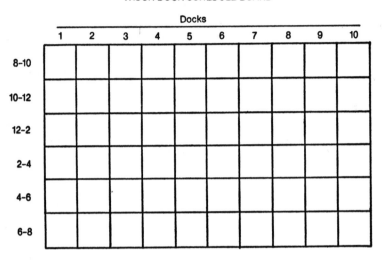

TRUCK DOCK SCHEDULE BOARD

Docks

	1	2	3	4	5	6	7	8	9	10
8-10										
10-12										
12-2										
2-4										
4-6										
6-8										

CRT SCREEN FOR SHIPPING

Ship Date	Order No.	Wt. Cube	Dest	Carrier	Time	Dock	OK
XX / XX / XX	XXX	XXXX	XXXXX	XXXX	XXX	XX	XX
XX / XX / XX	XXX	XXXX	XXXXX	XXXX	XXX	XX	XX
XX / XX / XX	XXX	XXXX	XXXXX	XXXX	XXX	XX	XX
XX / XX / XX	XXX	XXXX	XXXXX	XXXX	XXX	XX	XX

194

Most small parcel delivery services will provide drop trailers for major volume shippers. The picked orders, after they have been weighed and metered, can travel by conveyor from the picking lines directly into the trailers.

Carriers will also drop trailers for high-volume users. The shipper, of course, has to use warehouse personnel to load the vehicle. The total shipment will go on the basis of "Shipper's Load and Count." It should be noted on the manifest that the shipper's load and count will be considered as correct until the first break bulk transfer point, when the shipper must be notified of any errors.

Material will move from the warehouse storage areas and picking lines to the accumulation areas. The shipments must be verified prior to loading, perhaps at a CRT station on the dock. This will confirm that the shipment has been picked and is available for loading into the outbound carrier. As the shipments are loaded onto a trailer, they should be confirmed with the Bills of Lading or manifests for the shipment. This information can then be keyed into a CRT terminal at the shipping dock.

DISPATCH SYSTEMS

Warehouses that are delivering material to end users, such as a supply or maintenance storeroom, can use the same procedures as noted above. The order will be processed by the Open Order File and a picking document prepared showing the dispatch station and schedule that will be used to deliver the material to the end user. These shipments will be accumulated for loading into the delivery vehicle.

WILL CALLS

Users or customers will often pick up ordered material to defray transportation costs or to speed up delivery. If prior notice is given by the user, the order can be scheduled into the picking system, and the material can be placed in an accumulation area to await the customer or user's arrival. The shipper can enter the CRT with the customer or user number, find the proper shipment and the location on the shipping dock, and then move the material to the dock for loading on the outbound vehicle.

For small warehouses the customer or user will magically appear at the will-call counter and demand the products or items needed. This is an example of direct-order entry onto a CRT as shown in Chapter 3, except that the customer or user cannot be delayed.

This type of order is entered in the CRT, the inventory checked and location determined, and a combined picking and shipping document prepared. While the customer waits, the stock clerks or pickers assemble the material and bring it to the waiting customer. The computer system must have quick response time and be interactive between the Customer, Inventory, and Location Files so that the transaction can all be accomplished in a few minutes.

MECHANIZED WEIGHING
AND METERING

Equipment is available for automatic weighing and metering of small shipments. The shipment is placed on the scale and the proper location code or zone entered; the equipment weighs and costs the shipment and prepares the shipping meter label or shipping manifest for the shipment(s).

COMPUTER DETERMINATION
OF SHIPPING WEIGHTS

A more sophisticated system uses the computer to compute the shipping weight using the weight data for each SKU in the Product Master File. As the order is entered and processed, each line item is weighed out, the weights of all the line items are totalled, and the Bill of Lading can be made in conjunction with the picking documents. (Of course, the carriers will check the accuracy of the weights used to ensure that they are within a normal degree of error.)

PREPARATION OF MANIFESTS
AND BILLS OF LADING

The computer can be programmed to prepare Bills of Lading and packing lists for shipments and manifests for combined shipments.

This can be accomplished when preparing the picking document. Figure 11-5 shows a multipart picking, customer, and Bill of Lading set that can remain with the material as it

FIGURE 11-5 Combined Picking and Shipping Documents

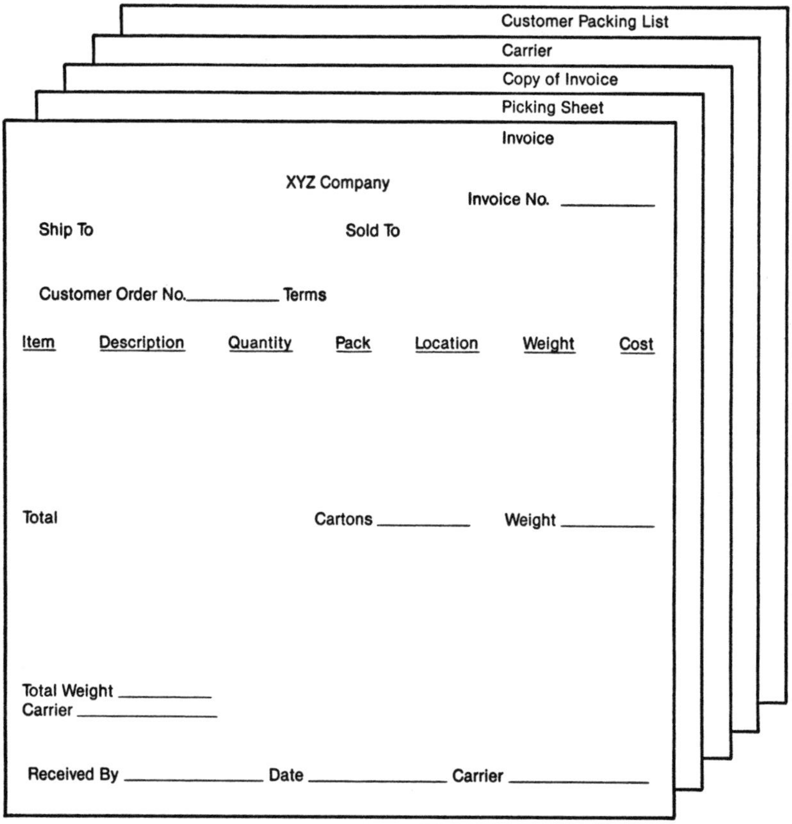

is picked, packed, and shipped. This is called preshipping the material and works very well if the inventory levels are accurate and the picker picks the proper material without error.

Many warehouses, however, must weigh the final shipment before preparing the transportation documents. If this is the case, a CRT and a printer should be on the shipping dock to prepare these documents when the physical material and picking document are placed on the dock. Figure 11–6a shows this system.

TRANSPORTATION RATES

Rates for most parcel services are readily available and can be updated in a computer file in the warehouse. Equipments are available that will allow automatic determination of these rates.

Rates for private truck fleets and contract carriers are also generally straightforward, as there are relatively few destinations and the charges should be directly available.

If the company has a small customer base, the updating of LTL (Less-Than-Truckload) and TL rates (Truckload) are easily obtained and the file can be maintained by warehousing personnel.

For warehouses that are shipping nationwide to many locations, however, there are many rates to be maintained. A service bureau that maintains rates can be incorporated into the computer system to supply the rate structure.

ALLOCATION SYSTEMS

There are some warehouses that bring in material and directly allocate it to users, customers, or other warehouses. This is usually the case where a master warehouse is supplying a number of warehouses with replenishment stock.

Another example is retail stores being supplied from a mother warehouse. As material arrives, it is allocated to the store or warehouse that needs it. The computer is supplied the total receipts of the SKU. It then allocates this quantity to the

FIGURE 11-6a Bill of Lading Preparation by the Computer

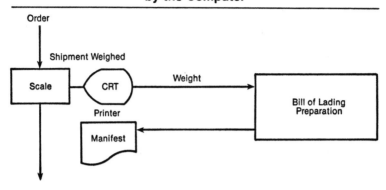

FIGURE 11-6b Allocation of Receipts Direct to Shipping Docks

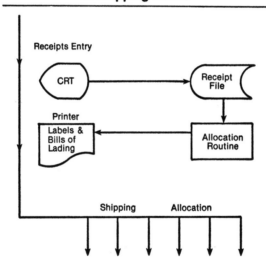

various customers or users based on an algorithm based on sales usage and the inventory status of the user points. The proper amount of material can then be physically moved to the accumulation area for the particular store, warehouse, or user. Figure 11-6b shows this system.

Physical equipment is generally incorporated into this type of system with automatic sorting devices and optical or laser scanning systems.

CHECK SHEET FOR SHIPPING
AND TRANSPORTATION ARRANGEMENTS

Figure 11-7 shows the check sheet for this chapter on shipping and transportation arrangements. The key elements here are to integrate the necessary lead time for carrier schedules with the scheduling of the orders from the Open Order File considering:

Delivery requirements of the customer

Personnel levels in the warehouse

Potential pooling arrangements

FIGURE 11-7
Check Sheet for Shipping
and Transportation Arrangements

Open Order File
    Designation of weights and/or cube
    Scheduling of shipments by ship date
    Designation of pooling codes

Open order scheduling of shipments based on:
    Shipping date
    Destination
    Availability of equipment
    Availability of labor

Pooling system

Dock CRTs and printers

Will call handling

Dispatch system

Mechanized or automated weighing and metering

Computer designated weights for metering

Preparation of Bills of Lading
    Manifests
    Packing lists

Transportation rates

Allocation system
    Inbound receipts
    Allocation algorithm
    Physical facilities

12

Job Enrichment
and Employee Satisfaction

Historically, the warehousing function has been considered as a lower level type of employment. Warehouse personnel were considered as just lift truck operators, or a kind of human robot who picks orders, packs orders, ships orders . . . dull, monotonous, nonthinking jobs. Of course this stereotype conception of warehousing was never quite true; however, like all myths it has persisted to the present day. The introduction of advanced materials handling equipment (both mobile and storage) with advanced electronic controls, the recognition by management that their warehousing facilities and personnel are a very important segment of the business, the rising cost of warehousing, and the recognition (by some) that warehousing is a direct cost and directly affects the bottom line have combined to explode this myth and in the process have upgraded both the status and the duties of warehousing personnel.

DUTIES AND RESPONSIBILITIES
OF WAREHOUSE PERSONNEL

Receiving. The receiver transfers "title" on possibly thousands of dollars worth of merchandise every day from

201

common carriers, vendors, or company-owned production facilities. The receiver must ensure that the materials received are in proper condition and that there are no overs, shorts, or damaged materials. The receiver must have personal acumen in dealing with various truckers and other people associated with the distribution and transportation function.

The receiver also has the responsibility for ensuring that the material ordered is, in fact, the material received. In real life, this means that the receiver must have a knowledge of the purchasing and replenishment functions. The computerization of the purchasing and replenishment function will further require that the receiver have the capability to transfer the physical movement of the goods to the computerized control over the goods.

Inspection. Inspectors have the responsibility to inspect and certify that the thousands of dollars of product is the proper product, will be on-specification for the intended end use of the product, and will not have the potential for errors that could lead to costly lawsuits. An off-specification or misidentified item can create difficulties both for the end user and for the production operation, if the company is involved in a manufacturing and assembly operation. It is much better to ensure that the proper product has been received in the warehouse *prior* to storage of the item in the warehouse so as to prevent any difficulties later.

Storage and rewarehousing. The storer has the responsibility for storing millions of dollars worth of inventory in proper and accessible locations and is also responsible for the proper utilization of hundreds of thousands of dollars worth of space. Every item in a warehouse must be accessible, or else, what good is it, if when it is needed it cannot be located? This can lead to customer service problems, as well as misstating available inventory.

The storers also have the responsibility and authority for rewarehousing material in the warehouse to maximize the utilization of the cube in the facility.

Picking. The pickers or order selectors in a warehouse have the responsibility to pick the items required by the customer or user in an efficient and accurate manner. Pickers do not generally have much authority over which items to pick, but they do have the important responsibility associated with accurate selection of items for customers, which makes for happy customers who will continue to be customers.

Packing. The packers are responsible for the proper protection of the items for shipment to customers. Here, judgments quite frequently must be made on the placement of the items within the shipping container and the proper dunnage or wrapping material to protect the items. The packer can "overpack," causing higher costs in packing material, transportation, and time. The packer can also "underpack," causing shipping damage to the items, which incurs additional costs, but more important, an unhappy customer. Notices that announce to the customer, "Jane Doe packed this package," can be an incentive for pride in packing.

Shipping. The shippers have the responsibility to transfer customer orders or company-owned material to common carriers or other outbound vehicles. Errors here can be of great financial consequence to the company, especially if additional product is shipped without proper authorization. Outbound shipments must be properly identified with the customer identification so that any loss or claim can be reimbursed through the common carrier or transportation company. Shippers are responsible for millions of dollars worth of material going out of the warehouse.

It can easily be seen that the warehouse employee is not a human robot, but has the responsibilities and authorities to provide accurate and proper use of the resources of the company.

The computer can provide an effective tool for the performance of the warehousing duties. Data can be made available to the employee for each of the warehousing functions and increase efficiency in performing the needed tasks in handling millions of dollars of merchandise.

UPGRADING THE DUTIES
OF WAREHOUSE EMPLOYEES

The warehouse employee must be made an integral part of a dynamic system that includes the computer for data processing and dissemination, advanced electronic controls, materials handling equipment both for storage and for movement, and advanced techniques for handling and shipping products.

The computer will force warehouse personnel to have specialized training to handle the functions for which they are responsible. Job satisfaction will increase as it is recognized that the warehouse personnel have an important position to play for the total productivity of the company. The increased specialization required by advanced equipment for the control and the physical operations of the warehouse will also increase job enrichment for the warehouse employee.

AVAILABILITY OF PERSONNEL

We are rapidly entering an era of advanced specialization in all functional areas of business. Indeed, the times dictate that business streamline inefficient operations or go out of business. The computer will control the mundane clerical operations and will also control and operate mechanical pieces of equipment. Warehouse personnel must be hired and trained to meet the new challenges and opportunities offered by a computerized warehousing operation.

Present warehouse employees are excellent candidates for meeting the needs of a computerized warehousing operation. They know the warehousing operation. This real life knowledge (gained only through experience) plus *good* training will provide an unbeatable warehousing operation. As the decline in the physical efforts of the warehousing function increases, warehouse personnel will be required to think and to accept more and more responsibility and authority. The pride in which individuals undertake to do their jobs will be important as errors will now be more costly. Gone are the days when, if a lift truck broke down, it created only a slight inconvenience. With advanced technology, complete operations can be halted, which can be extremely costly. Warehouse personnel must therefore be selected on their sense of pride and responsibility in doing a job and not on muscles.

RESPONSIBILITY AND AUTHORITY

In the past warehouse personnel have been given responsibility for the various functions associated with warehousing but generally have not been given much authority for how the job function should be performed and very little authority over the scheduling of their work efforts. With the advanced computer scheduling of the work involved in the warehouse, and with electronically controlled mobile, storage, and picking equipment, the worker will have more responsibility and authority in the scheduling of activities that make up the total function associated with warehousing.

The assignment of responsibility and authority to the warehouse staff will provide a more satisfactory job environment.

In the past 50 years the trend has been for people to want to have more responsibility, which implies additional authority, and people want to use their brains. The use of the computer in each of the warehousing functions will allow people to have the opportunity to use their innate capabilities to improve the operation, rather than being stuck with the dull routine operations associated with warehousing.

THE COMPUTER AS A TOOL
FOR THE EMPLOYEE

We see how the computer can be used to provide information on the work to be accomplished and the locations of material in the warehouse; it also provides a feedback on the performance of the employee, both in productivity as well as in accuracy and performance terms. The computer will allow the employees to concentrate on their performance rather than on clerical or physical operations that are required in present-day operations.

Computers can be programmed to be "user friendly." The employee can consider the computer as a friend that eliminates the drudgery and calculations that are typical of warehousing operations.

In receiving, for example, the purchase order for the shipment that has been received can be displayed on a CRT screen for the receiver to check the proper identification of the purchase order number and the identification of the proper material that was ordered.

In storage, the computer can identify all of the unoccupied cells for the storer so that the worker can select the proper location for material to be stored. With the use of light pens and optical scanning equipments, the burdensome paperwork required in present-day operations can be eliminated.

Picking can be accomplished by using CRTs that identify the item to be picked and the quantity to be picked. This eliminates the picker's wasting time juggling pieces of paper.

The computer will not only provide data information for each of the warehousing functions, but will provide a more satisfactory work content for the employee. Employees must be allowed to use their decision-making abilities; the computer and other advanced equipment will enhance their capabilities and enrich the work content.

PAPERLESS WAREHOUSE

In developing a computerized warehousing operation using CRTs, printers, and optical-scanning and bar-coding reading equipment, the amount of paper necessary to be handled in a warehouse is minimal. In a well-designed computerized warehouse operation the computer and other advanced electronics will aid the warehouse personnel in performing the warehouse work elements properly and efficiently. Burdensome writing and reading of pieces of paper will be eliminated. Time will be well spent on the business of the warehouse, which is to satisfy customer needs for the product of the warehouse while minimizing the cost of the operation and maximizing the utilization of the resources, both human and mechanical, to accomplish these objectives.

In a computerized warehousing operation the people employed must be willing to be responsible for their jobs and accept the authority over the function that they provide for the warehouse to accomplish its mission of receiving material, storing it, picking it, packing it (if necessary), and shipping it using advanced materials-handling equipment and storage techniques that are integrated with the computerized system to provide the warehouse employees with the data and work schedules they need.

13

Warehouse Performance Reports

Performance reports for warehouse control purposes are an operating necessity and should be directed not only upwards in the organizational structure but also downwards to the operating personnel responsible for the day-to-day operating functions of the warehouse.

Performance reports should be developed on a timely basis for both the service mission of the warehouse and for the cost performance of the facility. Service performance reports encompass:

> Order on-time service report
>
> Fill-rate or completeness-of-order report
>
> Accuracy of orders filled

and reports for cost performance are:

> Productivity of personnel by warehouse function
>
> Space utilization
>
> Budget for the warehouse

as well as the allocation of costs to product lines, customers, or user charges if appropriate to the warehouse mission.

Reports should be built up on shift performance, day-by-day for weekly summaries, and then week-by-week for monthly summaries, then month-by-month for quarterly summaries, and so on for each fiscal or calendar year.

Performance should be tracked on a time schedule to indicate whether performance is improving or decreasing so that action can be taken to reverse decreasing performance trends or to continue high performance.

ORDER SCHEDULE
PERFORMANCE

The order schedule performance report defines the warehouse's performance in meeting customer delivery needs in terms of time of shipment. When an order is received into the sales or marketing system the customer will usually indicate a desired date for receipt of the product. The scheduled ship date from the warehouse should allow time for transmittal of the order to the warehouse, order processing, picking, and intransit time to the customer.

Except for valid emergency orders, this lead time must be allowed for, for proper operation of the warehouse. Sales will often promise immediate or ASAP delivery; these are invalid scheduled ship dates—the real requirements for delivery should be determined from the customer or user. Conflicts between sales and the warehouse should be resolved by setting up the proper lead times from order entry to ship date and should be adhered to by both sales and the warehouse.

The scheduled ship date is the date entered in the Open Order File for shipment from the warehouse. This date is then compared with the actual ship date from the Confirmation of Shipment Routine to determine whether the order was shipped on time or not.

It should be noted that back orders are considered as *new* orders for scheduled ship date purposes, and no date can be entered in the scheduled ship date field unless there is assurance when the material will be received.

Most warehouses should be geared to meet customer demands within one week. In fact, most customer service-oriented warehouses should be geared to a 24- to 48-hour demand cycle.

The following information on the status of orders, from the Open Order File or Work Scheduling Routine, should be capable of display on a CRT screen. Hard copy reports should also be generated by the warehouse computer system, if necessary.

> *Orders not shipped by scheduled ship date.* This should include the standard work minutes for each order. This listing will indicate those orders that should be expedited in the warehouse and show how much labor is needed to bring the warehouse up to scheduled performance.
>
> *Orders shipped by date with standard work minutes or hours earned.* This report should show the number of orders, the number of line items, the total pallets, cartons, inner packs, and pieces shipped. It can also include the total dollars shipped for accounting purposes and total pounds shipped for transportation purposes.
>
> *Weekly, monthly, quarterly, and year-to-date summaries* can also be prepared, either manually or using the computer information.

Figure 13-1 shows the CRT format or print-out format for the reports. Distribution of those reports should be to the order-picking and -packing supervisors for updating data display charts in the picking and packing areas. Illustrative graphs for reporting performance to the warehouse personnel are shown on Figure 13-2. These graphs should be updated every day. Poor performance might be shown in red and good performance in green. Good performance should be rewarded with a pat on the back by supervisors while poor performance should provide the basis for action with the warehouse personnel to improve performance.

ORDER FILL RATE
PERFORMANCE

This performance report shows the number of line items that could not be filled because of out-of-stock conditions. It is really a measure of performance of the inventory control func-

FIGURE 13-1 Shipment Schedule Performance Reports

	ORDERS NOT SHIPPED			Date xx/xx/xx
Scheduled Ship Date	Order or Invoice No.	Customer	Work Min. for Order	Comments
xx/xx/xx	xxxxx	xxxxxxxxx	xxxxxx	xxxxxxxxx
xx/xx/xx	xxxxx	xxxxxxxxx	xxxxxx	xxxxxxxxx
xx/xx/xx	xxxxx	xxxxxxxxx	xxxxxx	xxxxxxxxx
xx/xx/xx	xxxxx	xxxxxxxxx	xxxxxx	xxxxxxxxx
Total			xxxxxx	

		ORDERS SHIPPED					Date xx/xx/xx
Order or Invoice No.	Line Items	Pal.	Cases	Pieces	Dollars	Wt.	Work Min.
xxxxx	xxx	xxx	xxx	xxx	xxx	xxx	xxxx.x
xxxxx	xxx	xxx	xxx	xxx	xxx	xxx	xxxx.x
xxxxx	xxx	xxx	xxx	xxx	xxx	xxx	xxxx.x
Total	xxx	xxx	xxx	xxx	xxx	xxx	xxxx.x

tion over the inventories in the warehouse that might or might not be under the responsibility and authority of the management of the warehouse.

The measurement should be taken at order entry, when the order is allocated to inventory. The measurement here is line items on orders that cannot be filled, whether cancelled or not.

In some order entry systems, especially for consumer goods, a measurement of pure demand for inventory items should be taken. A customer can request an item, but if it is not in stock will withdraw the demand without a formal order. This is a real demand on the system and if the item was in stock, there would have been a sale, or fulfilled demand. A separate procedure has to be established to measure this "pure" demand.

The daily report of unfulfilled orders due to stock shortages should list the SKUs that were out of stock and the number of line items that could not be filled because of the lack of stock.

The daily report of orders received, showing total line items, will form the basis for determining the percent of line

FIGURE 13-2 Illustrative Graphs for Warehouse Performance Reporting

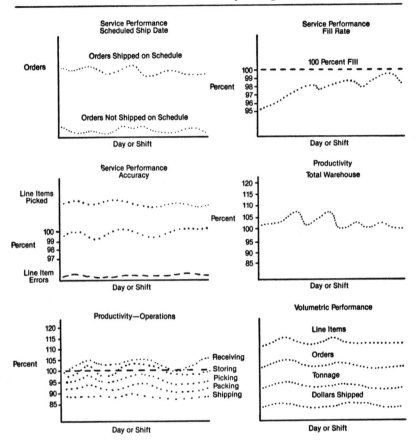

items received that could not be filled. This is a percent of line items not shipped to the total line items received.

Of great importance here is the type of SKU that is out of stock. If a fast-moving high-volume item is out of stock, it will create many line items that cannot be filled. If a slow moving item is out-of-stock, however, it will not have anywhere near the effect of a high volume SKU. (Figure 13-3 shows an illustrative out-of-stock report.)

If a warehouse is consistently out of stock of high-volume fast-moving items, this fact should be emphasized to the inventory control function and to higher management.

Figure 13-3 Daily Report of Out-of-Stock Items and Accuracy-of-Performance Report

DAILY REPORT OF OUT-OF-STOCK ITEMS

SKU	No. of Line Items	Quantity	Fast or Slow Movers	
xxxx	xxx	xxxx	x	
xxxxx	xx	xx		x
xxx	x	xx		x

ACCURACY OF PERFORMANCE

	Total Picked			Errors		
Picker	Orders	Line Items	Units	Wrong Line Item	Over Pieces	Under Pieces
xxxx	xxxx	xxxx	xxx	xx	xx	xx
xxxx	xxxx	xxxx	xxx	xx	xx	xx
xxxx	xxxx	xxxx	xxx	xx	xx	xx

The service level in a warehouse should be between a 95- and 100-percent fill rate. As shown in Chapter 4, the inventory control function should be able to forecast, inventory, and procure material to allow the warehouse to fill 98.5 percent of the line items received.

The Fill Rate Report should be submitted upward and, if the warehouse itself is responsible for the forecasting, procurement, and control of inventories, downward. Then this report, and the related graphs, should be released to the inventory clerks with the appropriate response from warehouse management.

ACCURACY OF ORDERS FILLED

This performance report is prepared using the inputs of the picking and shipping inspection function as to the errors made in picking orders. The report should also accumulate (from the Confirmation of Shipment Routine to the Open Order File) the total orders, line items, pallets, cartons, inner packs, and pieces shipped. These should be summarized for each picker reponsible for filling the order. The report should be by picker and show the total and the number of errors in line items and the picked quantities indicating whether the mistake was in the wrong line item or overages or underages in quantities. This report and the related graph for the pickers is also shown on Figure 13-2. This is a key graph for the picking function to show the pickers of management's concern about customer service.

Complaints with regard to customer order accuracy should also be plotted on the graph to indicate the feedback from the customer when errors are made. Remember to publicize good letters from customers too!

PRODUCTIVITY OF PERSONNEL

These reports come directly from the Warehouse Productivity Routine outlined in Chapter 7. The shift report will show the standard hours earned during the shift for each function of the warehouse. It can, if desired, be by name of the employee. The comparison of standard hours earned to actual hours paid can be prepared by the computer and presented in the report or can be calculated manually. The daily report should be given to supervisors of the functional areas involved, for example, receiving, storers, pickers, packers, shippers, and so forth.

Graphs in the functional areas should indicate the daily status of productivity to show the improvement or decreases in productivity over time. (These are shown on Figure 13-2.)

Other reports that should be incorporated into a warehouse productivity system could include:

Absenteeism reports by warehouse employee

Vacation schedules

Tardiness reports by warehouse employee

SPACE UTILIZATION

The space utilization performance report can be made when needed by the Space Utilization Routine as outlined in Chapter 6. This report should be made frequently when space is at a premium, and probably monthly during other times of the year. This report should be submitted to management executives to show how the warehouse space asset is being used. It should be provided to the storers involved in the warehouse and plotted on a graph as shown in Figure 13–4.

A good warehousing operation should utilize about 80 percent of the available storage cube. A higher utilization of cube generally indicates that there is congestion in the warehouse and labor productivity will suffer because of the lack of accessibility of each item to the warehouse employee. A less-than-80-percent utilization of the available cube usually indicates that the warehouse has too much space for the inventory levels in the warehouse.

Storage in a partially used warehouse should be confined

FIGURE 13–4 Space Utilization Reports

	Total Cube Available	Total Cube Used	Percent Utilization
Total Warehouse	XXXXXX	XXXXX	XX.X
Pallet Storage	XXXXXX	XXXXX	XX.X
Shelf Storage	XXXXXX	XXXXX	XX.X
Bin Storage	XXXXXX	XXXXX	XX.X

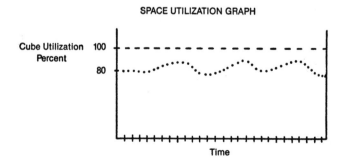

SPACE UTILIZATION GRAPH

to the forward or picking end of the warehouse to minimize travel distances of storers and pickers.

BUDGET FOR THE WAREHOUSE

A typical budget for a warehouse operation is shown on Figure 13-5. We shall not delve into budgets to too great an extent except to say that the total budget can be put on the computer,

FIGURE 13-5 Warehouse Budget

	Budget	Actual	Variance
Supervision	XXXX.XX	XXXX.XX	XX.XX
Clerical	XXXX.XX	XXXX.XX	XX.XX
Labor (total)	XXXX.XX	XXXX.XX	XX.XX
Unloading	XXXX.XX	XXXX.XX	XX.XX
Receiving	XXXX.XX	XXXX.XX	XX.XX
Inbound inspection	XXXX.XX	XXXX.XX	XX.XX
Storers	XXXX.XX	XXXX.XX	XX.XX
Rewarehousing	XXXX.XX	XXXX.XX	XX.XX
Replenishers	XXXX.XX	XXXX.XX	XX.XX
Pickers	XXXX.XX	XXXX.XX	XX.XX
Packers	XXXX.XX	XXXX.XX	XX.XX
Outbound inspection	XXXX.XX	XXXX.XX	XX.XX
Shippers	XXXX.XX	XXXX.XX	XX.XX
Loaders	XXXX.XX	XXXX.XX	XX.XX
Overtime	XXXX.XX	XXXX.XX	XX.XX
Vacations	XXXX.XX	XXXX.XX	XX.XX
Fringe Benefits	XXXX.XX	XXXX.XX	XX.XX
Total Labor	XXXX.XX	XXXX.XX	XX.XX
Occupancy Cost	XXXX.XX	XXXX.XX	XX.XX
Depreciation (or lease)	XXXX.XX	XXXX.XX	XX.XX
Space	XXXX.XX	XXXX.XX	XX.XX
Equipment	XXXX.XX	XXXX.XX	XX.XX
Power	XXXX.XX	XXXX.XX	XX.XX
Lighting	XXXX.XX	XXXX.XX	XX.XX
Air conditioning	XXXX.XX	XXXX.XX	XX.XX
Maintenance	XXXX.XX	XXXX.XX	XX.XX
Material Costs	XXXX.XX	XXXX.XX	XX.XX
Corrugated and packing supplies	XXXX.XX	XXXX.XX	XX.XX
Pallets	XXXX.XX	XXXX.XX	XX.XX
Office supplies	XXXX.XX	XXXX.XX	XX.XX
Etc.	XXXX.XX	XXXX.XX	XX.XX

with inputs from the payroll accounts, depreciation or lease accounts, and all of the small charges that are made. The budget report should be made monthly and variations explained both for good or bad performance.

Budgets should be developed based on work standards for each of the labor components of the warehouse taking into account the productivity of the warehouse staff and seasonal peaking that occurs.

Monthly variances from budgets should be explained. Volume variances should be the major reason for additional costs due to increased orders through the warehouse operation. Other reasons for variances from the budget might be:

Additional semiproduction operations

Change in work consist—larger or smaller orders

Additional SKUs

ALLOCATION
OF WAREHOUSE COSTS

An important area for computerization is the allocation of costs to product lines for distribution cost accounting. This is necessary if a company or institution is to show the distribution of expenses involved in a product line. Some profitable product lines carry nonprofitable lines because of the distribution expense involved. This allocation of costs can be made by proper coding in the productivity reports and in the space utilization reports, if the item number includes product class.

For public warehouses, the assignment of costs must be determined and billed to the customers both for space and labor. By assigning customer codes to space assigned and orders processed, the computer can provide space used and labor used for each customer.

End-user charges for material drawn from stockrooms can be included if there is a cost assigned for each SKU. This cost file is updated when receipts come in with the current cost of the item.

Figure 13-6 shows illustrative reports for allocation of

FIGURE 13-6 Allocation of Warehouse Costs

		Labor	Space	Total
Total Cost		xxxxx	xxxxx	xxxxx
By Product				
A		xxxxx	xxxxx	xxxxx
B		xxxxx	xxxxx	xxxxx
C		xxxxx	xxxxx	xxxxx
By Customer				
1		xxxxx	xxxxx	xxxxx
2		xxxxx	xxxxx	xxxxx
3		xxxxx	xxxxx	xxxxx
By End User	Material	Labor	Space	Total
xxxxxxxxxx	xxxxx	xxxxx	xxxxx	xxxxx
xxxxxxxxxx				
xxxxxxxxxx				
xxxxxxxxxx				

costs to product lines, end users, or customers for space and labor used.

Generally, the warehousing costs associated with a product group, customer class, or end user are readily identifiable for labor and space, and the cost of the material or product. The allocation of other costs—supervision, clerical, and other overhead items—can be more difficult, but these costs are of minor importance for the total allocation of costs.

CHECK SHEET
FOR PERFORMANCE REPORTS
FOR THE WAREHOUSE

Figure 13-7 shows the check sheet for this chapter. The major elements that must be accomplished are to define those performance criteria that will show the performance, both good and bad, of the warehouse workers so that improvements can be made for service levels to customers or users, costs of the operation, and the utilization of both space and labor.

FIGURE 13–7
Check Sheet for Performance Reports
for the Warehouse

Standards of performance—service
  Scheduled ship date
  Fill rate
  Accuracy
  Damage

Standards of performance—costs
  Receiving
  Inspection
  Storage
  Rewarehousing
  Space utilization

  Picking
  Packing
  Shipping

  Semi-production operations

Collection of performance data
  Work performed
  Schedule—shift, day, person

Computation of performance

Reporting of performance
  CRT screens
  Logic diagrams
  Reports and graphs

14

Implementing a Computerized Warehouse System

"Look before you leap."
"Faint heart never won fair maiden."

IMPLEMENTATION STEPS

Implementing a computerized warehouse system requires the following steps:

1. Develop the necessary *design factors* for the warehousing operation. This requires the collection of data that will quantify the warehouse input, output, and internal operations that are required for the particular nature of your warehouse operation.

2. Determine and *evaluate the options* open for improving the warehouse operations and determine the return on the capital necessary for adding equipment and controls for the operation.

3. Develop the *computer system specifications* for the new warehouse in terms of screen layouts, file formats and capacities, input and output formats, and the internal interactivity and routines that will be required.

4. Determine the *computer capacities* for the computer system and the necessary number of CRTs, capacity of the CPU, memory

requirements, and the number of printers and other peripheral devices such as modems, data scanning equipment, and so on.

These first four steps will define the warehousing and computer control systems for the operation. The next steps are implementing the final design to have a sound, functioning operating system.

5. Procure, install, and debug warehouse operating equipment, recognizing where interfaces with the computer system will be important.
6. Procure the computer hardware and peripheral devices.
7. Program the computer.
8. Test and debug the computer system.
9. Final systems test of the computerized warehouse system.

TRAINING

In the implementation of a warehouse computer system, one of the most important steps that must be taken during the total project is the training of the warehouse work force in new methods, equipment, and procedures. If the warehouse personnel are not proficient in computer equipment and procedures, they must be trained in advance of the installation of the equipment.

It is important at the start of a warehouse improvement program, that the objectives and framework of expected improvements be presented to the warehouse employees and their inputs solicited for the new system, equipment, and procedures. This up-front attitude will alleviate any misgivings of the employees on what is going on in the "front office," which can affect their careers and earning capabilities.

As the implementation progresses, the employees should be kept informed and training sessions held for those employees who will have key positions in the new system. Courses in computer operation, the installation of CRTs and computer games, the sending of employees to seminars, and the presentation of in-house seminars should be considered as vehicles for training the employees in the new system.

In a labor situation where an adversary relationship exists between labor and management, this close cooperation will be difficult compared to labor and management that are working well together. If there is an adversarial relationship, the challenge will be to gradually eliminate it so that by the time the new system is installed there will be a cooperative attitude between labor and management. Adversarial relationships between labor and management are disappearing and are an anachronism in these times.

DOCUMENTATION

Another major area of concern prior to delving into implementing a warehouse computer system is the need for documenting the project schedule, the results of analyses, the decisions made, the procedures, equipments, the operating plans, the programming, and so forth, that must be accomplished so that all parties involved in the design are on the same track.

Documentation means the writing of reports, the minutes of meetings, system specifications, computer programs, and the like. This documentation must be rigorously adhered to if the project is to be a success.

DESIGN FACTORS

The design factors necessary for the definition of a warehousing operation are:

Product classes.   The classes of products or categories of materials that will be contained in the warehouse. These classes or categories are dependent upon the mission of the warehouse and the types of materials that will be contained therein.

Stockkeeping unit definition and quantification. Every different and discrete item in the warehouse is a stockkeeping unit and must be defined as to:

Catalog number

Description of item

Package

Dimensions and weight of package

Any peculiar characteristics (The Product Master File in Chapter 4 defines these characteristics)

Pareto analysis of stockkeeping units. This analysis indicates the characteristics of the stockkeeping units in terms of sales demand or usage in physical units so as to determine the categories of:

Fast-moving items accounting for 80 percent of the volume

Medium-moving items accounting for 15 percent of the volume

Slow-moving items accounting for 5 percent of the volume

This information will be necessary in the development of the warehouse operating procedures, layouts, and equipment.

Customer order characteristics. This must be accomplished for both the computer requirements and the warehouse picking requirements and consists of developing frequency distributions for:

Line items per order. The number of items a customer will order.

Picking units per line item. This is the quantity that the customer or user will order of the item and must consider the package size that the customer will order.

Customers or users defined. The number of customers and their ordering patterns, service requirements, locations, and so forth, must be quantified.

Procurement or production sources. The number of sources and how the material will be replenished to the warehouse. The lead time and cost characteristics for the stockkeeping units in the warehouse will have to be defined by dealing with the procurement or production scheduling function. It is important that the implementers of a warehousing system have "hands-on" knowledge of the replenishment system.

Receiving and shipping modes of transportation. The quantification of how material will be received into and be shipped out of the warehouse. This includes the development of rail, truck, or other modes of transportation and the number of receipts and shipping vehicles per day.

Seasonality. The seasonality characteristics of the business—the highs and lows that can occur during the year, month, or week must be quantified. The effect on inbound and outbound characteristics, and perhaps the product line must be established.

Forecast growth. The expected growth of the throughput of the warehouse should be defined for the *next five years* by each year, indicating the pessimistic, most likely, and optimistic growth estimates for the company or enterprise. The effects on SKUs, number of customers or users, customer order characteristics, inventory levels, and production and procurement sources must be defined.

It has been said that with the proper definition of the problem 90 percent of the work has been accomplished. This is true in the design of a warehouse system. Just properly quantifying the throughput of the warehouse will give indications as to the proper solution to the final system.

EVALUATION
OF WAREHOUSE OPTIONS

Various equipment, methods, and operating plans can meet a given warehouse requirement. These must be quantified and investments and potential labor savings developed. Figure 14-1 shows the relationships between the various options and the reduction of labor expenses.

FIGURE 14-1 Evaluation of Warehouse Options

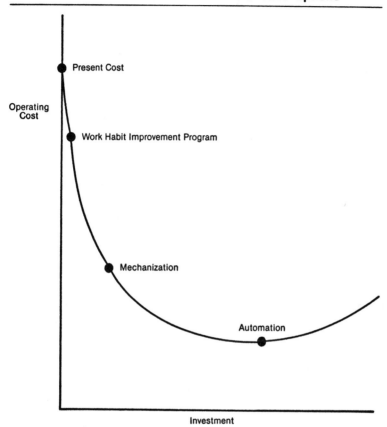

WHIP (Work Habit Improvement Program). This minimum investment program can reduce the labor requirements of a warehousing system by having the proper methods and discipline that are necessary for maximum utilization of personnel.

Mechanization program. This option requires the investment in mechanical equipment, such as driverless tractor-trailer trains, conveyors, forward picking lines, and the like, to reduce the work content while providing a proper return on investments.

Automation. This option requires high levels of investments to minimize labor content in the warehouse. The potential investment should be defined for a highly automated system that would minimize labor costs.

The return on investment should be quantified for each option. Option 1, the Work Habit Improvement Program, will have an instantaneous savings with no investment except for the time required by warehouse management and first-line supervisors to improve the operation. The Mechanization Program should provide savings that should allow the investment to be returned in one to three years. The Automation alternative usually requires a longer payback, but should be considered in some situations.

DEVELOPMENT OF COMPUTER SYSTEM SPECIFICATIONS

Once the decision has been made on the degree of mechanization or automation of the warehouse, the development of the computer specifications can start. The decision might be to computerize an existing good warehousing operation, or that there could be changes in equipment to allow for more effective utilization of manpower or space. The computer system specifications must be integrated with the final warehouse operating plan.

The computer system specification should include:

Screen layouts for each routine. The screen layouts should be developed and approved by the operating personnel involved in the system. As the computerized warehousing system is an interactive system with warehouse operating personnel who supply and use information, these screen layouts will be a major part of the operating system for the warehouse.

File formats for each of the pertinent files for the warehouse control system. The files most commonly used in a computerized warehouse system are:

Open Order File. This is necessary for the input of customer or end-user orders and for preparation of picking documents. It will also be necessary for prepicking of orders and scheduling of the picking operations in the warehouse.

Inventory File. This is interactive with the Open Order File and allocates orders to inventory, thereby maintaining an accurate and timely inventory status.

Location Matrix File. This file shows the location of all inventories in the warehouse.

Customer File. This could be required for customer-based warehousing operations. The identification of each customer with shipping and billing addresses and shipping instruction are parts of this file.

Back Order File. This file will be necessary if there is a significant number of back orders in the system.

Product Master File. This file is necessary for the SKU identification and specifications that could not be included and maintained in the Inventory File.

Transaction File. This file contains an audit trail of material movements through the warehouse.

Standards File. This file maintains the standards for the warehouse operation and is used to determine the productivity of the warehousing functions.

Operating Files. These are the files that will be used to maintain information for input, output, or operating subroutines.

Descriptions and data transactions for each routine. These are:

Order entry

Allocation of inventory to orders for each line item on the order

Customer interface with order entry

Location interface with Inventory File

Receiving routine

Location of material routines

Rewarehousing routine

Order scheduling

Replenishment of forward picking lines

Cycle counts and physical inventories

Material transfers

> Receiving to inspection
> Inspection to storage
> Storage to forward picking lines
> Order picking from stock to orders
> Packing, if necessary
> Inspection of picked orders
> Dock locations

Etc.

From this development of the routines, the interactivity chart and transactions can be developed for the routines and the files of the system. Figure 14-2 shows this interactivity and transactions.

Development of algorithms for each routine.   The formulae, logic diagrams, and instruction sets must be established for each of the routines.

Operating instructions for the users.   This is a natural outgrowth of the design of the interactive system and must include what the operators and warehouse personnel will do to interact with the computer system. These operator instructions should be developed with the warehouse personnel in mind and must be tested in training sessions with the operating personnel.

Development of the hardware for the system.   Based on the file sizes, the number of transactions, and the locations of the CRTs and printers in the warehouse, and other data transmittal devices, the hardware requirements can be developed showing:

Number of CRTs

Number of printers and output capacity

CPU size and memory

On-line memory

FIGURE 14–2 Interactivity Chart of Files and Routines

Routine	Customer File	Open Order File	Product Master File	Inventory File	Back Order File	Location Matrix File	Transaction File	Standards File
Order Entry	X	X	X	X	X	X		X
Customer Identification	X	X						
Allocation of Order to Inventory		X	X	X	X	X		
Back Orders		X		X	X			
Stock Location		X		X		X		
Receipts				X	X		X	
Inspection				X			X	
Storage				X		X	X	
Rewarehousing						X	X	
Replenish Picking Lines						X	X	
Order Picking		X		X		X	X	
Order Packing		X						
Shipping		X		X				
Cycle Counts						X	X	
Productivity						X	X	X

Note: The Transaction File entries for Receipts and Inspection refer to the } Purchase or Production Order File.

Off-line memory

Data transmission equipment

Etc.

Costs of EDP equipment.   Costs can then be developed based on vendor quotations and the availability of existing hardware.

Various options can be involved here. As in the automation and mechanization of a warehouse, the incremental computer costs for applications that will save clerical and warehousing labor can be developed and the return on investment calculated.

A total "ideal" computer system might not provide the economic savings to justify the system. Major savings can be made, however, from a portion of the computer controls that could be established.

PROCUREMENT AND INSTALLATION OF WAREHOUSE EQUIPMENT

Bids for warehouse equipment should be obtained and evaluated based on cost, the service of the vendors, quality of the equipment, and so forth. It must be remembered that the low bidder might not be the best overall vendor for materials-handling equipment.

Detailed schedules of installation must be made and vendor-installed equipment must have performance guarantees. For a complicated system, a Gant or PERT-chart might be appropriate. Total systems responsibility must rest somewhere. A project manager should be assigned with total responsibility and authority for the system implementation.

Figure 14–3 shows a typical schedule for a combined warehouse improvement program and the installation of a computerized warehousing system. This is a PERT-type chart and shows the activities and events that must take place for a quality implementation. It is on a time frame to indicate the time requirements for the system installation.

A major factor in the installation of equipment is the training of workers in using the new equipment. Warehouse

FIGURE 14-3 PERT-Type Implementation Schedule

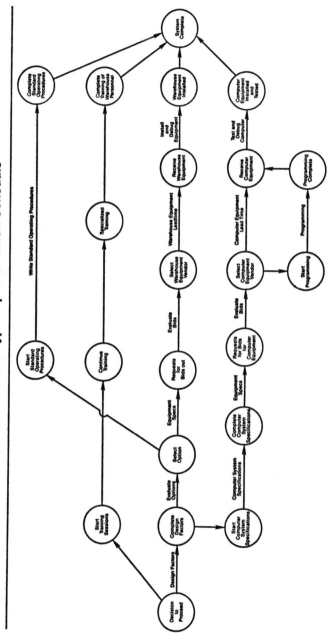

personnel could be pretrained by vendors and go to vendor's schools if needed for proper operation of equipment.

Another factor in the implementation of a system is the assurance that the installation will not disrupt the operating requirements of the warehouse. This means that detail planning must be accomplished for the transition period between the old and the new system.

PROCUREMENT
OF COMPUTER HARDWARE

Competitive bids should be obtained for the computer hardware for the warehouse control system. These bids should be reviewed for price, capacities, and service. Service is the key element for the smaller warehouse. The computer will be controlling the total warehousing operation and must therefore have a minimum downtime.

Systems responsibility must again be defined so that no interfaces between computer hardware and equipment are ignored.

PROGRAMMING THE COMPUTER

Programming can proceed once the decision is made on the computer hardware, its capacities and capabilities. Software packages might be available for many of the functions that are desired for the warehouse, or the programming must be accomplished by in-house or contracted programmers.

The key issues here are to establish a realistic time frame for the programming that will have key points when the program is tested using live data.

TESTING AND DEBUGGING
THE COMPUTER SYSTEM

The computer system must be tested and debugged prior to final completion. The present system must continue until the computer system proves itself out.

CHECK SHEET FOR IMPLEMENTATION OF THE COMPUTERIZED WAREHOUSE SYSTEM

Figure 14-4 is a check sheet for the activities necessary for implementation of a computerized warehouse system. The major elements here are:

Determining the design factors

Evaluating warehouse system options

Developing the computer system specifications for the warehouse operations

Evaluating the computer system options

Procuring warehouse equipment

Procuring computer equipment

Programming the computer

Installing warehouse equipment and computer equipment

Testing and debugging the system

FIGURE 14-4
Check Sheet for Implementation
of the Computerized Warehouse System

Design factors
   SKU definition and analysis
   Customer order characteristics
   Customers
   Seasonality
   Forecast growth

Evaluate warehouse system options
   WHIP
   Mechanical equipment
   Automation

Computer system specifications
   Screen layouts
   File layouts
   Algorithms and routines

Computer equipment requirements
   CRTs

FIGURE 14–4 (continued)

CPU
Memory
Printer
Peripherals

Warehouse equipment bids

Computer equipment bids

Install warehouse equipment

Program computer

Install computer and peripherals

Test and debug computer

Train workers

Standard operating procedures

Index

Pallets (*cont.*):
  example, 114–15
  forward pick line replenishment, 116
  heights, 114
  picking of, 115–16
  storing, 114–15
Paperless warehouse, 206–07
Pareto's law:
  curve, 57 *fig.*
  discussion, 56–58
  mover types, 56
  statement, 55
Performance reports:
  contents, 208–09
  check sheet, 219 *fig.*
Personal productivity, reports:
  discussion, 214
  example, 212 *fig.*
Personal time, 120
Personnel of warehouse, duties and
    responsibillities:
  availability, 204–05
  high-tech, 205
  inspection, 202
  orders vs. actual receipts, 202
  packing, 203
  picking, 203
  receiving, 201–02
  responsibility vs. authority, 205
  rewarehousing, 202
  shipping, 203
  storage, 202
  upgrading, 204
Picking documents, 21, 29–32, 34
Picking path determination:
  discussion, 143–44
  example, 143 *fig.*
Picking/shipping documents, 197 *fig.*
Pooling routine:
  CRT screen and pigeonholes, 190 *fig.*
  discussion, 189, 191
  holding time for orders, 191
  pigeonhole approach, 189–91
  volume vs. weight, 191
Popularity picking, 138
Private trucking, 192
Procurement interface:
  chart, 65 *fig.*
  files for, 64–65
  nature, 64
  push vs. pull, 63–64
Procurement lot size and economic
    production run, 67 *fig*
Product master file, 40 *fig.*
Production scheduling:
  discussion, 66

file, interface with, 80–81
lead time, 66
quantities needed, 66–67
Productivity reporting:
  check sheet, 129–30 *fig.*
  codes, 126–27
  control chart, 128 *fig.*
  sorting, 127
  at standard, worksheet, 127
Productivity standards, 111–12
Programming computer, 232
Purchasing interface, 65 *fig.*

Quality assurance audit trail, 163 *fig.*
Quality assurance, computer controls:
  inspection, 161
  orders inspection, 161–62
  picking, 161
  receiving, 161
  storage areas, 161
Quality control and assurance in ware-
    house:
  accumulation before shipping, 160
  checkpoints in warehouse, 156 *fig.*
  check sheet, 165
  clerical errors, 160
  customer complaint log, 160
  cycle counts, 158
  damaged materials, 158–59
  error log, 159–60
  inspections:
    inbound, 157
    levels, 157
    problematic materials, 157
  packing, 160
  picking, 159
    inspection, 159
  reasons for, 154–55
  receiving, 155
  replenishment of forward picking,
    159
  rewarehousing, 158
  shipping, 160
  storage, 158
  unloading, 155
  warehouse as bank, 155
Quality control inspection:
  cursory, 83
  detailed, 84
  random, 83
  receiver's, 83
  technical, 84
Quality control specifications for
    SKUs, 85 *fig.*
Quarantine areas, 158